TH

SECRET

SAUCE

Superscale your business
and empower your talent with
empathetic leadership

SAM SMITH

R^ethink

First published in Great Britain in 2023

by Rethink Press (www.rethinkpress.com)

© Copyright Sam Smith

To every entrepreneur who has ever taken a risk, tried to do something different, tried to change things for the better and challenged the status quo.

Most of all, to those who have always looked after their people, valued them properly and given them a chance. You are my inspiration.

To my little one, Aoife, who continues to inspire me every day with her confidence and passion for life, and the way she thinks so differently. She says she isn't going to be an entrepreneur, but let's see.

Contents

Foreword

I'm often asked the question, 'How did you get started?' While it's a fun conversation, it misses something important; success in business is determined by what happens much later in the journey. The first million is fun and exciting. An idea takes shape and customers start to respond by spending actual, real money. A small team forms and, despite feeling hopelessly out of their depth, they juggle things into existence.

Suddenly, the business gets some computer systems, weekly team meetings are attended by more people and you can log in and see the numbers grow. Then comes the day that you realise you're on track for that magical 'seven-figure target'. What you don't realise is that the game has only just begun. If you want a business to become valuable, profitable and impactful, you're going to have to scale up. You also don't realise that everything is about to break.

The vibe of your close-knit team is going to be challenged, and there's more than likely going to be fights and problems. Flawlessly looking after customers is actually dependent on a few things that don't scale, and you're about to let some people down – they're going to write nasty reviews and it's going to hurt. You're about to be side-swiped with a legal issue that could be existential. You are about to hire someone who seems amazing who is going to damage your culture. Some of your best people are going to leave. Someone you trust is going to betray you.

There's a reason that bigger businesses are worth millions; it's not easy to build them. It almost never happens. In the UK, less than 40,000 out of 5.5 million businesses grow to a team size of 50-plus people.[1] Included in that 40,000 are corporations and their spin-offs, as well as many old and established businesses. When it all boils down, about one in 200 entrepreneurs will scale up.

If it were easy, everyone would do it and it would no longer be valuable. It's not easy, but there are strategies and playbooks you can learn that make it possible.

Sam Smith knows how it's done, and she's captured great ideas in this book. Sam is one of the few entrepreneurs in the UK who has started a business, grown it

---

1.   J Andrews, *UK Business Statistics and Facts 2023* (Money, 2023), www
     .money.co.uk/business/business-statistics, accessed 4 April 2023

past £1m per year and then kept growing the revenue up to £1m per week. She then floated her company on the London Stock Exchange and successfully handed the day-to-day operations over to a leadership team.

Along that rarely trodden road, Sam had to figure out what changes for a business that does £1m per year and one that does £1m per week. In this book, she captures her ideas and strategies that made the difference.

This book is not for everyone. Not many people get to the point of needing a book like this. Many people don't even want to scale their business, but for those who are ready and willing to take their business on an exponential leap, this book will be read and re-read many times.

At the core of this book, Sam gives you rare gems of advice on building culture. A culture that overtakes the founder and attracts the type of people who build real value. A culture that scales.

Daniel Priestley, CEO, Dent Global

Introduction

You're heading towards your first million and you don't know what's hit you. You're working so hard and taking on every role under the sun – finance, HR, sales, making the tea – because you haven't got the cash to hire anybody. You're at the start of something that could be big, but you might not be even sure what it is yet. You might not have had time to think about how much your business can grow, or what your unique style as an entrepreneur is – there's just too much to do.

If you've ever had a child, you might recognise this feeling from that first moment when you take your bundle of joy home. The good news is that it doesn't last forever, and it never feels that hard again. Eventually, your child sleeps through the night, and goes to nursery and then school, just as, eventually, you will get past your first million, get some proper revenue and recruit some of the help you need.

Believe it or not, even before you get to your first million you can commit to supercharging your growth. As you work towards that million and beyond, you can build the team you need, share your vision with them and create the culture that will make them the best they can be as they grow with you.

Culture, rather than solely monetary reward, is the driver that people are looking for in the modern working world, particularly the younger generation. A truly inclusive culture that makes your people feel uniquely valued is what will set you apart from the competition, and cultures that properly align staff's interests with that of their leaders will create better businesses, build long-term sustainable growth, and can transform UK entrepreneurship.

A good culture has been crucial to me since my early career, when I was about to qualify as a chartered accountant at a big firm and was interviewing for corporate finance and research roles at various large institutions. I had gradually been realising that I didn't enjoy the process-driven culture of large companies, where individuals had little chance of achieving change and did not always feel valued.

At the time, a close friend was diagnosed with cancer and I wanted to visit her in hospital after a (thankfully successful) operation, but instead, I was asked to stay at work to finish a late-night audit as was frequently required. I decided there and then that it was more important for me to go and see my friend, but much bigger than that, aged 24, I decided that I was not prepared to let that happen again, to me or anyone who worked for me.

It was a moment that altered the course of my career in a positive way. It made me realise that being valued by an employer is about the small things. It is at these moments that you can make a team member feel valued or you can lose them. It made me realise that inclusion and good culture are about knowing what the individual needs and demonstrably caring about that. If businesses put their people first, what might be achieved? That is the type of culture that builds loyalty, trust and enthusiasm, but, most importantly, it can also scale your growth.

That moment changed my career path away from large corporations and, instead, I joined a private client wealth manager, J M Finn & Co, to lead a brand-new division providing corporate finance and fundraising services to UK growth companies. I was excited to build a division from scratch. Everyone else thought it was extremely risky and wondered why I wasn't going down the more traditional route, but I didn't. I was determined to follow my path, with principles of fairness, inclusion and treating people well. I wanted to build something different and prove that focusing on people and culture can lead to profitable growth.

My growth journey began with, at its heart, a special culture that treats people as the key asset that they are, a culture that helped me scale finnCap from a start-up division into an independent business listed on the London Stock Exchange, with £52m turnover and generating nearly £10m of profits.

We didn't even have a new idea at the start, just a different way of treating people and clients, and a belief that this would create a better business. We continued to win market share from our competitors because of our culture, which became our USP, and we set new standards for financial services. Today, I work with companies that want to scale up using people, culture and vision, helping them to create a culture that scales and, as a result, builds better businesses.

Your business can grow as mine did if you have a growth mindset. Everything is possible. You just have to start by committing to growth on a bigger scale than you might have believed possible, setting targets that excite you and painting the big picture for your people.

Market conditions will always be a factor beyond your control, but over the twenty-four years of finnCap's growth, our market (the small/mid-cap area of financial services) didn't grow – it actually shrank. While a series of obstacles and events rattled our competition (the collapse of Northern Rock followed by the general financial crisis, which came just after we had bought out our parent company), we overcame these adversities and grew even stronger than before, because we had created a solid, connected team who were all pulling in the same direction. You can achieve this, too.

The Secret Sauce will help you create a culture that will attract the great team that you'll need for your growth journey, and that will keep them motivated. I will talk you through how to hire the right people, give them a financial and emotional stake in the business, and empower them to be your future leaders. Through this culture, you will make people feel valued, happy and, therefore, productive. This is how you keep people generating ideas and going the extra mile when the market gets tough, so you can keep growing whatever challenges you might face.

You will hire better talent than you could expect to for your stage of development, and people who want to be part of your culture will seek you out because they know you will look after them. You will also learn to look after yourself on your growth journey, and relish it, while being your authentic self.

The opening chapters of the book will show you the importance of establishing a growth mindset that needs to be embedded in your culture from the start, and then help you set your growth trajectory. We will then look at how to set the vision for your growth journey and sell it externally and internally.

In Part Two, we will investigate the recipe for our 'secret sauce' – the process that creates a culture that scales. It's about adding some good E-numbers – our 6Es.

The first step is to assemble your ingredients: a vision that will **Excite** and inspire your team. You then need to:

- **Enrol** your people on that vision by making it mean more to them emotionally and/or financially, so you get their buy-in (Turning Up The Heat)

- **Engage** people in an inclusive culture so that they feel valued, and so that everyone is aligned with the growth journey and ready to go above and beyond (A Rich Mix)

- **Elevate** people to maximise their performance, spotting your future leaders and accelerating their path through the business (Extra Spice)

- **Energise** people to supercharge your long-term growth, turning the 'fizz factor' up and down as you need to. This is where having fun at work turns out to be in tune with your growth vision, and you can continue motivating your team when the initial excitement has died down, through good times and bad (Shelf Life)

- **Exit** people if you need to in a way that aligns with your culture and does not stifle your growth, making tough decisions to minimise any fallout for the rest of the business (A Slow Simmer)

All of this requires your constant attention to be focused on individuals and what makes them grow. As the CEO, most of it will fall to you, although it's important to ensure your managers are steeped in your culture.

If this sounds challenging, it is. You'll need to be your own growth champion as well as everyone else's, so you'll need to look after yourself, but this book will tell you how to do that, too.

PART ONE
BE YOUR OWN GROWTH CHAMPION

ONE

Your One-Way Ticket To Growth

Introduction

A culture that scales is driven by a great vision, inclusivity and finding and retaining great people, but, most importantly (and first), it is about a growth mindset. That is where a culture that scales begins. To keep a culture that scales at the core of your business, you need to pay attention to the 6Es. Let's look at these again:

Excite and inspire the people you want to lead on your growth journey.

- **Enrol** people in that vision.

- **Engage** people in an inclusive culture so that they feel valued and everyone is aligned with the growth journey.

- **Elevate** people to maximise performance.

- **Energise** people to supercharge growth and make it fun. A happy team leads to productivity and growth.

- **Exit** people in a way that does not stifle growth (part of managing your workforce strategy in a way that aligns with your culture).

First, you need to establish the growth mindset that needs to be embedded in your culture from the start. When setting out or when trying to scale a business, the mindset of an entrepreneur needs to be absolutely committed to growing. No ifs, no buts and no need for an exact plan about how to get there. Just a commitment that, no matter what, you will grow.

There was never a year at finnCap when I didn't think about how we were going to grow. Quite often, I didn't know exactly how we would get there, but I was happy to have that come later, and we would always find a way. What never left my vision was that growth was the only option.

There is always a way to grow, but you may not find it if you aren't set up for growth from the start. If you think of new geographies, new sectors and new products as the three key areas in which to scale, there is almost limitless potential. Once you set out on a path towards growth, options that you may not have thought about, or may not have seen as available to you before, will start to become visible. New products, new services, new sectors, new add-ons, new geographies and new people who have new ideas all start to present themselves when you start thinking bigger. Developing a consistent and committed growth mindset is the most underestimated part of growing a business, and also the most important. Yes, it is scary, and no, it isn't easy, but a shift in mindset is necessary if you are going to scale your business and ensure that growth becomes embedded in your culture.

From observing businesses you know, including your competitors and some in different industries, you will notice that some of them will have grown (some slowly and some very fast), some will have stayed where they are and some will have shrunk, or even gone bust. What those that grow have in common, is a CEO or founder who has set out a vision for growth, with growth as part of their mindset. As the CEO, you are the company's growth champion.

Grow your growth mindset

If you are fully committed to growth, and constantly thinking and talking about growth, you *will* scale your business.

When you set out a plan, no matter how big or optimistic it is, you increase your chances of success simply by saying, 'This is the plan, and we're going to get there'.

If you are a business that has just reached £1m turnover and you say, 'I just can't see how I'm ever going to get to £5m', you are not going to get to £5m. If you say, 'Right, we're getting to £5m,' even if you have no idea how, it then becomes absolutely possible.

In the early days of finnCap, when we were a small division, our first task was to cover costs with revenue and to start making a small profit that we could reinvest to keep the business growing. That early stage of trying to hit £1m revenue is always the hardest step because you're working so hard and taking on every single role. It's worth remembering that growing gets incrementally easier as revenue grows. Once you have got to £1m revenue you have done the hard part and proved that you have commercial potential. That is why venture capitalists and investors start looking at businesses at around £1m revenue, or certainly £1m of annual recurring revenue (ARR), because they have proved their commercial concept.

However quickly you want to scale is up to you, but the most important thing is to set a target. You don't need to know yet *how* you're getting to £500k or £1m, £2m, £3m or £10m; you just need to be clear that that's where you're going. The planning comes later but the growth trajectory is set. It's all relative: if you're at £200k turnover, £2m or even £1m seem far away, but you need to be thinking constantly about the next milestone on the journey and believe you can get there.

It takes almost the same amount of effort and energy to double revenue at each stage. That's why it takes a long time to scale a business, and it can't be done overnight. A lot of people get disheartened when they hit £500k revenue because they have already gone through many doubling journeys – but the next doubling journey will get you to £1m in revenue, and that will be no harder than getting from £250k to £500k. As you grow, you will build your skillset and the process of doubling revenue will get easier as the numbers get bigger.

THE FINNCAP GROWTH JOURNEY

After finnCap had hit £1m revenue, our next aim was to get to £2m. When we hit £2m, we aimed for £3m, and so it continued. We hit £1m revenue fairly quickly but it took much longer to hit £2m consistently, and then much longer again to hit £3m consistently; in fact, it took ten years from first setting up the division for us to achieve that, around the time we completed our buyout in 2007. The next target had to be more exciting and definitely beyond £1m increments, and we had reached a stage at which it was possible to scale that bit faster. Our next target was much more aggressive – we set out a plan to get to £10m revenue with a mission to become a market leader in the microcap company space, which was a small sub-sector within the growth-company space.

For us, the ten-year point was the right time to think about really scaling up, largely because we grew organically, reinvesting our own profits into the division.

We had raised no outside finance by this point, which may have made the process somewhat faster.

I grew at the pace that felt right for me and the business. Trusting your gut about the speed of scaling is important and will differ for each person and each business. It can come down to personal circumstances and personal choice, and how much external financing risk you are prepared to take. My choice was to keep reinvesting profits for the first ten years to build our proposition and learn how to do each part of the job. I was twenty-four when I took on the role of building the division, so I had a lot to learn! Scaling too quickly without acquiring the necessary skillset can lead to problems, so work at a pace that feels challenging but not out of control.

Your personal target beyond the milestones

As well as setting the next revenue milestone, it is important to keep in mind the bigger picture and your own internal, longer-term target. You may or may not choose to communicate this, but I always chose not to. It was my own personal aspiration, my ultimate goal, my real big-picture vision. My aspirations were so big as to seem far out of reach to most people, and potentially unachievable for the team, so it didn't seem to me helpful to communicate them. However, these aspirations were still fundamental to hitting the revenue milestone that had been communicated.

It is important to think constantly about the bigger picture, about what might be possible for your business. Whatever the figure you set for your internal milestone or target, it should be aspirational, and much bigger than where you currently are – at least double your current revenue, although it can't be so big that it is out of reach and therefore unbelievable. When I was presenting to the team about our £10m target (we had just reached £3m revenue, so £10m was our next stretch target), I was also thinking about how we could move past that and get to £50m. That was my own personal stretch target; the bigger picture, the 'where-could-we-really-go?' target, and that £50m had to be a possibility in my head.

If you're constantly thinking big, you will think differently and make different decisions because you're planning for future growth, and opportunities will arise that wouldn't otherwise be in your picture. You will see possibilities that you otherwise would not see, from who you might hire, to new products to add, to new geographies to enter. My £50m aspiration target made it possible for me to see things that made £10m achievable.

Having a bigger target makes things happen, and it becomes self-fulfilling. Throughout my twenty-four years as CEO, every time I met a mentor or a business coach, met with one of my CEO groups, listened to an inspiring TED Talk or heard from a business that had already done the growth journey, it made me think a bit bigger. I was constantly moving the growth dial as I realised what is possible. Spending time with people who have larger businesses and who inspire you to think bigger is important. One conversation can have a huge impact. I experienced this several times.

MY SCALING ASPIRATION BREAKTHROUGH

The biggest turning point for me, in terms of growth, was a conversation I had with a mentor, which materially changed the scale of my ambition. At a retreat for CEOs, I met one of my mentors who had been running and had just left a big investment bank. I was talking to him over lunch about how I wanted to use culture as a real driver of change in the advisory space, and how culture could move the business forward. At this point, we were at £17m turnover and a bit stuck. I was delighted when he got what I was talking about; that had a lot of weight because he had run a multi-billion-pound company, miles away from where I was.

During our hour-and-a-half lunch, he asked me, 'So what is blocking you from growth? Where do you think you could get to? Where is your largest competitor in revenue and is it possible, with limitless time, that you could get there?'

Then he asked some important questions: 'Where in your head have you got your endpoint? What is limiting you?' It was the first time I'd ever thought about those questions. My target of £50m revenue, which I had set for myself at around our £3m revenue mark, was my personal success marker. I believed that if I could get the business to £50m, I'd have done a great job.

He said, 'Well, that's your blocker. Do you think you could get any bigger than that? Take away timeframe, take away whether it's even you doing it, do you think this business, given an infinite amount of time, could grow beyond £50m?' And I said, absolutely it could, because our competitors had hit £200m revenue. Many global investment banks are at multi-billion-pound revenues, they have just added more services and more geographies and acted for larger companies. My mentor got me to see that it was my own perception of what I considered success, and what I considered an endpoint, that was blocking me. He said, 'You need to forget about this £50m target. You need to think way beyond that. The rest will happen.'

I left the lunch in Pall Mall and walked back to the City deep in thought. Was this the problem? By the time I got back to the office, I knew I needed to think that growing to £200m was now possible. I needed to revisit my £50m aspiration target even though we weren't there yet. The business had moved from £3m revenue a year to £17m a year, and my long-term vision and aspiration target had not changed. This was a problem, and this was why we were stuck. I was seeing far enough ahead to make £50m a reality, but I needed to see further. Within a few hours, my internal/aspiration target had grown to £200m. As soon as I removed the £50m target and thought much bigger, everything else fell into place. Obviously, I did not talk to the team about my £200m vision, but it was now there, firmly planted, and was my next aspiration target on the journey. We then broke through the £17m revenue level fairly quickly.

SCALING AND MARKET SHARE

Once you start to think that bit bigger, it opens your mind to how you can grow. This always involves looking at the current size of the market you are in and considering what's a realistic share of that market. For our first fifteen years, we were nowhere close to our target market share, so still had a lot to go for. It wasn't the right time to think about new markets. When we looked at how we could move beyond £50m revenue, it became obvious that we would need to look beyond our current market. We felt that we could achieve 10% of the current market, but moving above that would become extremely competitive and challenging.

The problem was how to grow revenue without the constraints of market share becoming too big and difficult. Our thinking moved to looking at complementary services that could be sold to the same clients as well as trying to increase market share in our existing market. Growing market share beyond 10% was too hard, but we *could* scale if we added another complementary service that no one else had. That change of thinking led to our first acquisition. If I hadn't changed my mindset about how much we could grow, that acquisition might never have happened.

Once I aimed for £200m in my head, I started looking at things differently. I didn't communicate that goal to anyone else, as I have said, because it was so far off, but following our acquisition in 2018 of a business that was generating around £10m of revenue, we revised our revenue plan from £50m to £100m, called Project Premiership. I talked of £100m as our new five-year target. This was a real stretch at first (and remember that it was still only half of the figure in my head), but as we hit £47m in one year, the £100m started to look much more achievable. That meant I started hiring in a different way because I wanted people who would take me beyond the previous £50m revenue target. I started seeing possibilities in my peripheral vision that I hadn't seen before. The window of opportunity, and therefore growth, had opened.

Find the headspace for big-picture thinking

I learned to think bigger from people who were a long way ahead on their scaling journey, who were used to thinking about what was almost impossible, and how it could become possible. It takes time to learn to think like that, and you need to put yourself in a position where you can think strategically and see the big picture. That's hard when you're growing. There's so much to do, because you're head of HR, head of finance, head of this, head of that. There's so much detail that you quite often get stuck in the weeds. It's so important to keep talking to people about the bigger picture, about the next stage, about what might be possible and what might be blocking you.

It is also important to have those growth discussions with yourself and others, and make sure you have time to be your own growth champion, because that's a job only you can do. If you make the time, it will lead to growth. Not spending the time slows growth.

You probably can't take time out to think specifically about strategy in the early days. I only started doing that consistently when we got to around £17m turnover. When you're scaling from there to £50m, and beyond to £100m, you have to think outside the box. It is part of your job to spend time looking for opportunities to set aside considerable time for strategic thinking.

In the early days, do whatever works for you to get your thinking time. Get away by yourself for a long walk or a swim, or chat to other CEOs in an environment that is not just about work. I used to get a lot of thinking done on long flights, in the days when phones didn't work on aeroplanes. I could switch off from the outside world and get my notebook out. Travelling to new places and getting some time out used to give me the space I needed to think about strategy and the big picture, and to come up with new ideas or to solidify what felt like the best next stage.

Start asking yourself, 'What's stopping this company from becoming really big?' There should be nothing that can stop you in the long run, even if there's an obstacle like a big competitor that will take time to work around. The important thing is to believe that it might be possible. As soon as you start thinking, 'I don't know how I'm going to do it, but it would be possible to buy something else, to double up, to merge with a similar business, to buy in a new geography, to add a completely new product line', then you are in your growth mindset and the potential for growth is infinite.

Growth takes time

Seeing ahead to something huge is actually quite hard. Good things, like scaling a business, take time. Most businesses take more than ten years to get to something significant. It took ten years for finnCap to get to £3m revenue, but in our second ten years, we grew to £50m+.

Amazon was founded in 1994 as a bookseller. They didn't think at the beginning that they were going to become a platform to sell everything. It turned out that they're an amazing aggregator. They can sell, they've got a platform, and they can deliver, and they can deliver fast. At the beginning and along the journey, you don't know where you're going to end up. What you do know is that if you don't think it's possible to keep growing, you won't grow. You won't find those opportunities. You won't find ever find your real game-changer moment like Amazon did.

Always be thinking about the next step, make it mean-ingful, make it challenging. Make it further than you can currently see. The opportunities will then start to present themselves. If you don't think big, you won't get bigger.

There will be a lot of imposter syndrome at every stage. It doesn't go away, and I have yet to meet a CEO who doesn't experience it, no matter how big they have scaled their business. Each step in the scaling journey builds confidence. It makes it that bit easier to see the next milestone, to look back at what has been achieved and realise that the shift in mindset is the most important thing. Set that next target. Don't worry that you don't know how to get there yet, and make it just that bit bigger than feels comfortable. The window of growth will open.

I always have to remember, and remind others, that there is no manual, no easy guide, to being a CEO. There is just a mindset and a set of problems to solve at each stage that builds your skillset. Learning from others is important, and building your own self-awareness and skillset is a must, but there is no shortcut and every CEO learns on the job. Remembering this can make it seem that bit less daunting and that bit less lonely.

Summary

Before you can start creating a culture that scales, you will need to establish a growth mindset and remove the barriers to growth you have already created by imagining that your respectably ambitious but attainable growth target is your ultimate goal. In fact, your personal target should be much bigger, even if you do not share it with anyone. Get help with thinking bigger from mentors, make sure you meet with more successful businesses, and allow yourself time for big-picture thinking.

Once you start to think big, you will attract the people and opportunities you need to grow, and see possibilities that you had not imagined before, perhaps outside the current constraints of your market.

Growth can take a long time, but the process will get easier and you will learn how to speed it up.

TWO
How You Talk To Your Team Matters

Your vision comes from you

When you are a growth champion and leading the growth mindset of your business, your aspirations are hopefully always one step ahead of everybody else's, and one step ahead of what you're prepared to share. You might think: 'I could get this company to a billion pounds. It might take me fifty years, but that's what's possible. I can see it.' The big vision that you share with your team can't be unbelievable, but it does need to be aspirational.

How do you then communicate your big vision to the team? How you sell the vision, how you talk about growth, how *often* you talk about it, how consistent you are, your tone of voice and your confidence, are all crucial to how your team will receive your message and therefore how confident they will feel about achieving your goal. Everyone will watch your every word and your every move, and even the tiniest things will get noticed. How you talk to your team absolutely matters, which means that your energy matters. You have to be constantly in the right frame of mind for successful growth, and you cannot afford the luxury of having a bad day. We'll look again at your responsibility for sustaining your business's energy in Chapter 7.

Once you have your vision, you have to get everyone on the journey, to commit to the goal that you're prepared to share, and to talk about it. Set milestones and talk about the next stage and how you're going to get there. You're driving the bus, encouraging people to leave their comfort zones and helping them get in the zone of growth, and they may quite often feel nervous about change. Change comes with growth, and although change can be difficult to navigate it is much easier when everyone is on board with achieving your vision.

Your team need to know that growing is the only option. This will drive behaviour and more than likely attract people who are motivated by working for a growing business. If growth is ingrained in your culture, it will encourage the team to look for opportunities, the journey will become more exciting and the required mindset will filter down and generate ideas. Opening up the idea of growth to everyone and including it in your culture will give you the maximum potential for ideas, which can come from everywhere and any-where, everyone and anyone, at any level. Ideas can be big game-changers or they can be small process improvements and seem insignificant. They are both as relevant as each other. Encouraging your team to be part of the journey will give you the best pool of ideas as you decide together what growth could look like. It is a team game – the more players, the faster the growth.

Step into the spotlight and share

Telling your team and the outside world about your vision, culture and growth plans, is a non-negotiable part of your role. If you're not a good natural speaker or, more likely, you don't like it or aren't confident, you need to learn. It is a skill that needs to improve as you scale. People (both your team and the outside world, including the media) will expect to hear from you as CEO; they want to hear from the real you, and hear what's driving you.

That doesn't mean you have to try to be funny, engaging and interesting; you aren't a comedian trying to sell out the London Palladium. You don't have to be an extro-vert. Your authentic style might be quiet and steady, but you need to be confident and sell something with vision and purpose. You need to be authentic to earn trust, and that means being utterly yourself, genuine and real.

For some leaders, especially many female leaders that I have met, the concern is often, 'How can I be confident that I am leading in my own way?' A lot of the time you feel that you need to sound and behave like a CEO, so you look at other CEOs and think you'll do it like them, but then you realise that, if you copy someone else, it's not going to work.

You need someone driving both your external and internal comms, and at the start that someone will be you because you will be doing everything. I did it for the first twenty-four years of our journey.

If you really can't learn to speak publicly with authenticity, you could delegate, up to a point, but only to a co-founder or joint CEO, if you have such a person. As you scale, you might find someone who is able to present to town hall meetings (large company meetings, ideally in person) as well as you, but you still have to be ready to answer questions which could come at any time. It's likely that, when you first need to do it, there's only you – and at some point you will have to do it yourself. If people aren't convinced that you believe what you're saying, they're not going to get on the bus with you, be that your team or potential investors.

Nobody is great at speaking when they start. I was sick twice before speaking to 100 people for the first time. You just have to start from whatever confidence level you are at and work on it. You *will* improve, and you can scale your skill as the company grows. Selling your vision to a larger audience is part of growing and is important to your scaling journey.

IT'S ALL ABOUT YOU: FIND YOUR INNER ORATOR

Once finnCap grew to more than twenty people and I couldn't get us all around a table to chat, I had to learn about public speaking. I was terrified, but I realised it was worth investing the time and energy to improve. It takes much more time than you might think: my first coach told me that one five-minute speech to staff should take a week of practice. You practice in front of the mirror, practice every single mannerism. What appears to be completely off-the-cuff will have been rehearsed within an inch of its life, but it will come across as natural, relaxed and unrehearsed. People who you think are brilliant off-the-cuff speakers are not – they just practice a lot.

Start training as your business grows until you are comfortable presenting to twenty people, then up to fifty. We grew up to 160, but I could present to 3,000 now. There is no end to the work you can do to improve your speaking skills. If you didn't have a business to run, you could work on it full time. For a while, you might spend more time on the message, the vision and learning to be an orator than you do on strategy and execution, though you can't let either priority go.

My training was a combination of reading books, watching videos and working with a range of trainers, including an actor/director friend. I found it helpful to look outside standard presentation-skills training. My breakthrough came at a three-day retreat hosted by comedians. By then, I was quite good at speeches but not confident, and so nervous I wouldn't sleep for a week beforehand. Confidence comes from being relaxed, extremely well prepared and able to be authentic.

We spent three days getting comfortable with telling stories about ourselves. There was a lot of improvisation, getting up and telling stories about the things that shaped us. To say I found it terrifying is an understatement, but I found my stories. My performance went to the next level and my authenticity and confidence shot up.

You have to get used to listening to the audience, following their cues. It's harder on Zoom, because there is no engagement, but, as with everything else, you can learn techniques – watch people who do Zoom presentations well, and work on a series of short, snappy presentations rather than one long one. You never stop learning.

Who do you need in the team next?

Building a business is a journey. You plan where you need to be in the next five years and who you will need. As you grow, the mix of the people you need on the bus – who you need to attract – will change. It's a great journey for most of those who join you, but not for all, and this needs to be constantly assessed. You might need to find some people a better seat on the bus – a role where they can flourish.

At every stage, identify your key team, your future leaders. Work out what they will need to be doing in three to five years' time and make sure they know that they are key to your vision. It is important that you tell your good people that you think they're superstars, where you can see them going within the business, and how that's going to work. People who are good at their jobs might seem confident, but sometimes they don't know how good they are and what they're capable of until you tell them. Think about how you will grow them into their role. It's much easier to bring someone along on the journey from the beginning than to add someone in a crucial role later, who might introduce a culture clash, or not understand the business.

In year two after our buyout (so, year twelve of our journey), we were experiencing a growth spurt and I had lots of heads of departments. I was thinking about what they needed to achieve over the following three to five years to get to the next level. I hired a coaching firm to review all the team skillsets, plus psychometric tests of my direct reports to see who needed what kind of coaching. When the results came back, unfortunately, pretty much none of them were going to make it through the next three-to-five-year stage of the journey in those particular roles. I needed to work with the coaching firm to make wholesale changes in a way that was going to keep the whole team happy, and I needed to work on what the ideal team structure would look like in three to five years in order for us to hit our growth targets.

Rather than saying, 'I need some different people,' I spent a long time working through how I could make people fit better. Some people took a step back or sideways from head of department, letting someone else take over while they focused on what they were good at. Inevitably, you will lose some people during processes like this, but that should be the last thing you want to do if it can be avoided (see Chapter 8).

While you're working on how to make people fit better into your company, don't forget those who already fit (the key team that we identified above), and make sure they get enough of your time. Review your key people on a monthly basis and check that you have spent enough time with them, or if you need to get something in the diary. (See Chapter 6 for reasons why that is important.) It's easy to forget people who are not causing problems, but if you're always spending time on problem people, you might miss those who will be helping you drive the bus.

Summary

How you communicate your growth culture is important for keeping people on your journey with you. If you don't have the required skills to paint your picture in others' heads, now is the time to learn.

Your external brand is what wins you customers and work, but also positions your culture in a way that will build your reputation and attract the people you need as you work out who you'll need if you're to get where you want to be in five years' time. Your internal brand, which we will look at in the next chapter, is what wins you your people and gets your team to embrace your culture.

THREE

The Journey Of Internal Comms

Why you have to do it

It is tempting to put internal comms on the back burner when you're busy. It's a lot of work, people might not notice you're doing it and you don't get a lot of credit for it. When you get sucked into day-to-day pressures, it's easy to forget about. Yet it is crucial, because it's what keeps your culture embedded throughout your organisation and keeps people on the bus.

As the external message attracts the people you want, the internal message retains and empowers them. The internal brand is key to people's first impressions when they join the company, and, in fact, as soon as they are interviewed and hired. It needs to be hard-wired into your induction process and, once they are aboard, it has to be inescapable.

How much? Who to? How often?

Research shows people only start to listen to something they are being told after many repeats, and, even then, they only start to *hear* it – that is, to really *understand* it and be able to act on it – after many more. My experience bears out what Sean Conner says in, *'Say It 7 Times: The art of overcommunication'*.[2] It has taken me at least seven times to get the team to start listening, and at least fifteen to get them really hearing what I am saying and therefore acting on it and helping grow the business. That means repeating my growth message a potential fifteen times before I get real buy-in across the group – that is, it means something to them that they can translate into growth.

Not only do you have to convey the message fifteen times to get it heard and understood, but you must also say it in many different ways to ensure everyone completely gets it, being mindful that everyone has different ways of absorbing data. A one-size-fits-all approach won't work. You need to activate the data-driven people, the visual people, the people who are a bit bored that day so aren't listening, those who deleted your email because they were busy, those who heard the first thing you said but missed the second and third

---

2. S Conner, 'Say it 7 Times: The art of overcommunication', *Medium* (16 May 2018), https://medium.com/unexpected-leadership/say-it -7-times-the-art-of-overcommunication-5d019b2c33d4, accessed 24 March 2023

because they were thinking about their deal. The list goes on, but you get the point.

It really is important to get that message across to everyone, but fifteen times is a lot, and it can get frustrating and even fairly boring. You've said it so many times, why aren't they getting it? It's easy to assume that your presentation wasn't good enough, or that you did something wrong, but the truth is that people are finding it much harder to focus and they are used to information being disseminated TikTok-style, in tiny hits.

If you want people to get behind your growth agenda, you have to keep repeating it in a way that they can hear or else they won't know what's happening and you won't get them on the bus. Once everyone gets it and they're all on the bus, the energy is like that of a rowing eight, a synchronised swimming team or an orchestra. If everyone is in sync, all going in the same direction, you go faster, perform better. That's what creates growth, performance, vision, excitement and energy.

If there's one person who hasn't quite heard, who is a beat behind the rest of the orchestra or the synchronised swimmers, you're going to come unstuck, and growth is going to be harder. To get everyone moving in the same direction and absolutely understanding where you're going, you cannot skip the internal comms work.

What are the key internal comms moments?

For me, that town hall moment when you sell the vision to your team in person is critical to scaling. It is vital at the start, but also important on an annual basis to reset the strategy, to focus on the new financial year, the vision, the goals and the priorities for the year ahead. I try not to cover more than three key take-away messages and reinforce those throughout the presentation.

We would repeat the town hall format every six months, as we reported half-year and full-year numbers, and update everyone on our progress. These sessions are much better in person and really set the tone for the year ahead. You need to be on your A-game.

One town hall every six months is not going to cut it, however. Regular reinforcement of the message in between times is key. Check after a town hall to see how much people have understood, and it's likely that you will find they need something else, and the something else will vary massively. Some will have taken onboard one point but not the rest, some will have got the big-picture message, others will have taken away very little.

What is the best format for your message?

Some people need videos, some will only watch short snippets, others are better at reading emails. Preferred written formats vary between age groups. Some want bullet points, some want data, some want chatty descriptions. Some only look at WhatsApp but can take in a lot of information that way.

How do you know what communication styles suit your people? You ask them, try things out, look at the stats and try again. There is no set process; people are people and every team is different. We learned that we needed to do monthly written and video updates together (they were each absorbed by 40% of employees, but by different people). We learned that we might need to send the same email twice with different subject lines to appeal to different people.

You might need to do one-to-one lunches or group breakfasts, ask someone else to repeat the message, have your targets on screensavers. Whatever you choose, the important thing is to keep checking if it's working, if enough people understood it. If not, you need to try something else.

Scaling is about trial and error: trying what works, trying something different, looking at what other people do and trying that, thinking outside the box and asking people for feedback. Don't let frustration and disappointment, which go with the turf, knock you off course. If you ask people when you're at the coffee machine whether they read an email and they haven't got a clue what you're talking about, don't get upset. You just need the self-awareness to understand and think, 'OK, no one heard what I said there,' or, 'Everyone hated that video. Let's just try something else.'

Listen when people are telling you something useful. If someone says, 'Oh, that was just a few minutes too long,' you can take that away. That little comment, which you wouldn't have heard if you hadn't asked, might mean you can engage another 20% of your workforce.

INSIGHTS COLOURS

There are many personality profiling or psychometric testing methods you can use to help you understand the communication styles that work best in your organisation.

We worked with the Insights Discovery® colour model. When people joined, we would complete their Insights Discovery profile, which expressed their personalities as a particular mix of colours, with their lead colour showing their most effective way of working. We shared this with their manager, but the individuals themselves found it interesting to hold a mirror up in that way, often finding out things they didn't know about themselves.

We used the colour profiles to work out how people operated, both under stress and when they were happy, and looked for patterns. We realised that greens were the people who wouldn't say much in a meeting, but they'd be thinking about everything. You would need to ask them directly, 'What are your thoughts on this?' or 'How did you observe this?' You can sometimes do this in the meeting, but it can be more useful to ask the question soon after. You'll get some amazing ideas, but they won't be able to voice the thought while they're still thinking it.

This is just one example of why you need to personalise your communication. In reaching out to people in their preferred styles, you'll not only get your message across more efficiently, but you'll make them feel valued as individuals, which will support your culture.

How do you make it stick?

Drilling in the message takes constant work. If something is not happening, it's tempting to say (or scream), 'But I said that!' You did, but no one heard it. Or worse, they heard but didn't understand it. You're not doing anything wrong. You simply need to keep repeating the message. You will have to help your managers understand this when they say, 'But I've told people this!'

I feel constantly that I am over-communicating, which Barack Obama says is impossible. At the same time, though, I never get to a stage at which I feel I have communicated enough, and I feel that I never would, even if I spent all my time on it.

Internal comms is one of the most important yet most overlooked jobs in scaling. When you start, it might be a big step to share what's in your head with even one other person. Another likely scenario is that there is just a handful of you, and you all share the same vision, and you are talking about it all the time, and you don't foresee when this will change. If you're in a small team with a close bond, it doesn't matter whether you're working remotely or in the same room. Because there's so much to do at this early stage, the moment when you have to change your communication style will creep up on you.

As soon as you grow past twenty people, you can't communicate as a group. It's not a given that everyone will hear the same message. When you scale past thirty, and then past forty, the dynamics shift again.

Each time you scale, you have to start disseminating information in a different way and your skillset as a leader needs to change, as we discussed in Chapter 2. When you need to talk about strategy, you will have a lot of people in the room at the same time, all eyes will be on you and you'll be under pressure to come up with something, deliver it well and still be yourself. You have to learn to read your audience and tell whether they are bored or engaged. Our business scaled at twenty people a year, so I was able to manage the changing communication skills required, but other businesses grow from a small team to 300 in a single year. The speed of the necessary improvement and investment in internal comms then goes up considerably.

We found that, whenever movements in goals and strategic priorities were not effectively communicated to the team, we had people issues. No one likes surprises. We therefore started a system to ensure that we communicated as much as we could about what was going on at board and executive-committee levels. Once we become listed on the Alternative Investment Market of the London Stock Exchange in 2018, it became harder to share some information, but key strategic themes could be covered.

To increase the chances of your message sticking, be disciplined about prioritising what to say and why. There will be times, after a great board meeting or a great strategy session, when your head will be buzzing with possibilities about where you can go next. Make it a habit to decide right away the most important thing to communicate to the team. What's the message? How could you communicate the next steps to sound out the idea? Don't try to communicate more than three points at once. Three really is the magic number. More than that and the team won't remember anything.

Who can help you?

In my time as a CEO, I never stopped thinking about internal comms. My top management team could say they were too busy generating business, but I couldn't. It seems like an easy thing to cut back on when you are scaling and you are under stress, but the more that is going on, the more important it is.

Work out who is good at talking to people, good at listening, who can be your eyes and ears, and help you understand whether something has landed. My PA did a lot of this in our early days. It could be your head of marketing, COO or CFO. These are the people you'll need as pulse checkers in the long term (see Chapter 7).

You need in-house culture champions, who will carry your culture forward as you scale, at every level in your company. If they're junior, they're still relevant; they will be the culture carriers for their group. In Chapter 8 we'll look in depth at how to develop those people.

Summary

Internal comms requires patience and flexibility as you drill in the message repeatedly for people who absorb information in many different ways. To get everyone moving in the same direction, you may have to tell your story multiple times. It is important to work out what the priority message is at any given point, and what is the right amount of information to deliver.

It can be frustrating when a message has not landed, and even worse when it seems to disappear, so find the people who can help you check what has been understood.

PART TWO
YOUR SECRET
SAUCE RECIPE

FOUR

Excitement: Ingredients

Embracing the vision

Your vision needs to excite your team. They need to understand it, get behind it and help you grow the business. It's your job as CEO to make your vision exciting and relatable in a way that gets your team's buy-in, which will drive the energy and enthusiasm needed to boost productivity and growth.

The vision needs to be clear, succinct and relatable to everyone in the team. Visions that inspire and excite come from what really drives you, as CEO. The most excitement is generated by communicating your 'why' – not only the business's 'why', but your personal 'why'. Having a great vision with a 'why' doesn't just help excite your team, it will also excite potential new recruits, new teams and new acquisition targets.

People will be excited by hearing you explain what it is about your vision that excites you, what gets you up in the morning, and what you would like to achieve and why. The more conviction and belief with which you can share your vision, the better. People are looking for someone real to follow and want to get to know the real you. Authenticity is key.

It might be that your initial vision is not your great, billion-dollar idea, just a place to start. It is enough simply to have the 'why' that is going to get you to the next stage and be able to communicate your excitement. As you grow, the vision will take shape and improve. Sometimes, it can take time to work out what is driving you. My personal 'why' increased in scope over time as the business and my own confidence grew.

A big vision isn't always apparent at the start, which doesn't mean there isn't one or won't be one. It might be that a gap in the market will appear that will reframe your vision. You may only be able to identify such a gap by working with competitors, talking to your customers and slowly realising that it's there. In fact, sometimes, gaps in the market appear just because you have committed to growth and started to grow. At the beginning, when our division was just starting out, we were doing something that was similar to other people, and it took a while to work out what we could do that was different. Not having a big initial vision doesn't mean that you can't grow. You just need to share the excitement of wherever you are: your initial vision and current mission.

Whatever vision you share, it needs to be all about growth. A public commitment to growth is inspiring in itself. People want to be involved with something that's growing and has momentum. In addition, more and more people want to be involved with something that has a bigger purpose than making more money and gaining market share. Those visions are not very inspiring. Your scaling culture will also attract people who are looking for this bigger purpose if you can work out how to articulate it and share your drivers and motivation.

Converting the vision to something relatable

Since 2022, part of the work I have done with companies is to help them visualise their scaling journey. Because I'm dyslexic, I see these journeys in images, in colour and in 3D, like an architectural model. When I read *Rocket Fuel* by Gino Wickman and Mark Winters,[3] I realised that entrepreneurs are divided into 'Visionaries' who see the big picture, and 'Integrators' who

3. G Wickman and MC Winters, *Rocket Fuel: The one essential combination that will get you more of what you want from your business* (BenBella Books, 2015)

make it happen. Sometimes, Visionaries are also Integrators, but that is unusual.

The Visionary aspect of the CEO's role is vital, but because the Visionary sees everything at once, in colour and bright lights, it can be hard for them to describe the growth journey in a way that enables their team to see it as clearly as they can, when they are always many steps ahead. Giving the right level of detail is important when setting out your vision for the journey. You need enough detail to make it real, but not too much for people to take in, or to seem too hard or unrealistic. Realising that my team couldn't see the same vision as me was a real turning point, since this meant I had to focus on bringing the vision to life and making it mean something to everyone in the team.

Painting the picture for everyone else can be quite a task. After you've spent a long time creating it by yourself (which can be quite lonely), you've got to convert it into an exciting story for everybody to hear, so they can see the picture you can see. That takes effort, and a realisation that what you see so clearly when you set out your vision might not be anything like what others see.

Storytelling is important for getting your team to remember your vision and to buy into it. It also means they get to know the real you better, which builds trust. The public speaking training that we discussed in Chapter 2 will help you hone your storytelling skills.

Don't forget that your vision and mission need to be relatable to everyone in the team, not just your senior team or your key revenue generators. I spent as much time selling my vision to the IT and reception teams as to my senior leaders. Making sure everyone can relate means that everyone will go the extra mile. People often forget that back office, middle office and administrative functions are key to good delivery.

How vision and mission evolve

Your overall vision for the business can be quite different to your current mission. Missions generally change over time as you reach your goals. Once each goal is achieved, you plan the next stage of growth and the next mission. For me, the vision didn't alter much, but the mission changed every few years depending on where we were aiming for next. The mission should be something that people can recognise as achievable, and should always be tied to your KPIs and shorter-term goals.

Your missions shift over time as you grow, expand your activities and acquire other companies or teams. Even if you acquire another company in a similar space, you've still got to combine two cultures. Every time you bring in a new team, things change. Do they agree with your mission? Is there anything to tweak? There is, generally, something that needs reviewing each time you grow, to make sure the mission is relevant to everyone.

THE FINNCAP VISION AND MISSION JOURNEY

Our initial vision was to provide a better level of service to small-quoted companies while maintaining our integrity. Our initial mission, however, was to be the largest adviser to microcap companies (quoted companies with a market cap less than £50m, that is, the lowest end of the quoted market). Once we achieved that mission, our mission upgraded – we then wanted to become a key adviser in the small- and mid-sized company space – but the vision stayed the same.

After ten years or so, we realised that our real USP was our culture, and at that point the vision became bigger, which enabled us to scale into other services.

At the beginning, I used the question 'Why are we doing this?' to get people excited. The answer to this question will usually point you towards your vision. Our initial answer was, 'Because we think that small companies aren't serviced properly by current competitors. We think they're getting a much lower level of service. They're getting the most junior person. They're not being treated in the way they should be, and they don't feel important.' Our real 'why', for about the first three to five years, was: 'To bring a level of integrity and a level of service to those clients that aren't getting it and make them feel special'. It wasn't going to scale us to £52m turnover, but it could take us from £3m to £10m, and probably beyond.

When we got to £17m turnover and our purpose was still 'helping ambitious companies grow', we got stuck. We realised that our real vision was 'To use our culture, which is our USP, to grow something big. To become a better adviser to small and mid-cap companies'. This became a vision for something much bigger, and we started to acquire.

When we bought Cavendish, which was our first outside acquisition, we changed our purpose to 'Delivering business ambition' to include other services, which helped us scale.

Why and when to set values

You need your values formalised and written down as your company grows to help you bring the right people into your organisation. At the beginning, it's likely that you will be doing all the recruiting yourself. When I started, I was hiring instinctively, looking for people who would be a great fit and who would work in the long term. As you grow, you'll no longer be the main recruiter, so you need to write your values down and make sure your managers understand them so that you keep hiring the right people. If you don't recruit on values, but instead recruit on skillset to solve your immediate problem, you'll hire the wrong people and your growth will stop. See Chapter 8 for more about developing your hiring process.

Depending how fast you grow, you might need to set your values quickly. For us, it happened at around twenty-five people. Before then, we had been small enough to be in constant communication and make decisions as a group.

Writing down your values gives you a focus for hiring and for measuring and rewarding performance. Once you have set your values, you have to live them: make them a focus in reviews, talk about what they mean, bring them to life regularly. Everyone in the team should be able to tell you the values of the company. A values-based culture is important to create a feeling of belonging.

Stay consistent when acquiring

Acquiring another business is a chance to get the outside world excited about your vision. It's important to keep talking about your 'why', about what your driver is, about what's important and about your company's impact beyond simply what you are doing. We consistently talked externally about our big vision over the years, so that we became known for it.

When we were looking at acquisition targets in the sustainability, diversity, inclusion, culture, consultancy space, and went to talk to those businesses, many of them were willing to talk to us when they wouldn't talk to our competitors or to private equity, because they were already aware of what our vision was. It was very much about trying to drive change and integrity in the marketplace, to provide a better service, to value people and to value clients in a different way. Everything our target companies saw us doing was in tune with everything we'd ever said. They saw that we were authentic, which meant that we had a good choice of acquisitions and we found the right one because they knew we were real and we'd been living our vision consistently for a long time.

When you're acquiring something, there needs to be a cultural fit and a mission fit. If you don't have those discussions at the beginning, it can come back to bite you. It's also worth asking whether there is a need to rethink your values when you acquire. You might have to work on some of your values if they don't align, as we had to do during our acquisition. There needs to be a consistency of vision, mission and values. This will lead you to be able to scale later if you want to acquire or bring in new teams, because they will know what you're about and they will trust you. As you expand your mission and vision and display it to the world, you create a narrative and that narrative can bring you massive benefits of scale.

Relatable milestones to ensure buy-in

When you achieve your mission, or you're getting close, what is the next stage? It's important to have your next goal ready. The vision itself is not the endpoint; as a leader, you constantly need to be looking for the next step towards your vision. When you're scaling and things are really getting busy, you have to think about it more and more, to make sure the excitement is still there for everyone.

To do this, the mission has to be broken down into milestones that are achievable. What are we going to achieve in one year? What are we going to achieve in the next three months? Constantly having three-month goals is important in making your ultimate vision relatable for the whole team.

It might be helpful to change your focus every quarter. If you want to win clients this quarter, for example, you can set a up fun campaign about it: what are your ideas? How could you bring clients in? How do you get the message out there? Once you've won twenty clients, say, you have to keep moving the vision on, so have a new thing for people to be excited about for the next quarter, or, if you're sticking with the same goal, present it with a new theme.

You need to break down your 'why' and your vision, as well as the mission, into manageable chunks with meaningful goals and KPIs attached to them that relate to everyone individually. Doing so will ensure that everyone knows how their input is affecting the progress towards growth and how their role relates to the vision. If they can't see how it relates to what their actual KPIs are and how they're rewarded financially, they will not feel connected to the vision and you won't grow as fast.

I used to spend a lot of time talking to our reception team about how they were the face of the firm, the first people clients see. If we were going to be about integrity and making clients feel special, and that's our USP, how do we do that? What is it about them walking through our door that makes them feel special? Suddenly, they saw what a valuable job they did and felt included in the vision; that they were contributing. They did make our clients feel special. We got so many great comments from our clients about how amazing they were, and they probably helped us win clients. That first contact instilled in clients a feeling of our culture, a sense that this is exciting, and this is why finnCap is different.

You might think that an entrepreneur is someone who says, 'I've got the best idea in the world and I'm going to write it on this piece of paper and then hire those people, and then we're going to go off and do it.' How would it be if you said, 'I've got the best idea ever, but I'm going to bring in a team, and then we are all going to build the vision together'? The vision is the same, but now you have the buy-in of your whole team by getting them to own the vision alongside you.

What can possibly go wrong?

When things change and seem chaotic, or there is a downturn or challenge, you have to step up with a revisited vision that reframes the difficulties as opportunities. The temptation is to keep your head below the parapet because it's all going wrong – the market is bad and everyone is scared that they won't get a bonus or will be made redundant – but this is when you need to refresh the vision in everyone's mind.

At times when markets were difficult, we managed to grow our business faster than our competitors in terms of numbers of clients because we were saying, 'This is the time to win the clients, to establish the next base from which to grow', while our competitors were doing the opposite. During the worst challenges, during a general financial crisis, we kept people committed to our vision. The following chapters will explain in more detail how we achieved this.

Summary

The way to growth is by constantly sharing the vision, checking you have everyone's buy-in and adjusting as needed. You have to constantly check your strategies and try new ones. As we saw in the previous chapter, you have to repeat, repeat, repeat.

The vision and mission have to be relatable to everyone in the team, back-office services as well as income generators. The vision should be broken down into achievable milestones and the mission should be tied to shorter-term goals and KPIs. Your mission will shift over time and your vision may need to be revisited or the story told in a different way. Your values should be set and written down once you are no longer a small firm, to make sure new hires know and are aligned with the values of the company. Consistency of values will help you stay true to your culture.

FIVE

Enrolment: Turning Up The Heat

Introduction

Once you've set an exciting vision, it's important to thoroughly enrol people in it. Enrolment is about turning a vision into something meaningful for the individual, whether emotionally or financially. Either will work, but if it means something to your people financially as well as emotionally, you will supercharge your growth.

Enrolment helps get buy-in from the team, so that the vision will mean more to them and they will go the extra mile to grow your business. You want people to deliver your vision, move it forward and make it a reality. They are more likely to deliver it if they're enrolled in it – affected personally – as well as being excited by it.

Building emotional connections

Real enrolment is about establishing an emotional connection which begins as soon as you meet a potential new hire. Everything that follows is a reinforcement of that emotional connection between them and the business and the vision. What happens in an interview matters. What happens when they accept a job offer and how you communicate before they join matters; a good connection in this period can really enrol people. The induction process is a key stage and is where enrolment really begins. Doing this well makes a big difference, and you only get one shot at it, so make it good!

One of the ways we helped people make a profound emotional connection with the business was to include them in our key decision-making. When we were coming up with our purpose, 'helping ambitious companies grow', everyone was involved in feeding in ideas. This collaborative process helped people feel enrolled in what we were doing and brought the vision to life. When we completed the buyout of finnCap from our parent company, J M Finn & Co, we needed a new name. The whole team came up with ideas and we created a shortlist, and we got everyone to vote for their favourite. The outright winner was finnCap, an idea that came from one of our analysts, but because everyone had been involved in the decision, it felt real and much more exciting for everyone and, as a result, we got real enrolment in the vision.

From the moment someone agrees to join you, you have to turn their intellectual decision into an emotional one. It's your culture that will reach them on the emotional level, especially in the first ninety days. If you succeed in making your employees enrolled at this point, it's more likely they'll be with you for the long haul.

We have been tweaking our induction process over twenty-four years. It starts as soon as people agree to join, to make sure we take advantage of every opportunity to make them feel enrolled. How do you bring them into the fold before they join? What happens the day they join? You need a process, and it needs to be executed well so nothing falls through the gaps. Each stage of the journey has to be part of the whole, to make recruits part of your journey right away. I would write personal letters to people weeks ahead of their start date, telling them specifically why I was excited that they were joining us and sharing the vision with them.

We would follow that up by sending them branded materials – a laptop bag, a water bottle – and a culture booklet about the company. We would make them feel that they belonged to something before they were in the building. We would set out specific events: that I would be sitting down with them for half an hour to explain the vision; that someone senior would take them for lunch.

The core of our process is an extremely detailed and structured plan for the first ninety days. We would give them the first three months' KPIs and monitor them closely. I used to give new hires, especially senior hires, a book by Michael Watkins, *The First 90 Days: Proven strategies for getting up to speed faster and smarter,*[4] and explain why the first ninety days are so important. We'd help them to fire on all cylinders and make sure they had some quick wins. There would never be a day when they wouldn't know why they were there or what they were supposed to be doing.

I would meet all new team members at the end of their first ninety days, which I found to be the point at which the best ideas came. That was the point when they could still compare us to their previous firm, we hadn't become their regular environment yet, but they had been there long enough to have a good view of the business and have ideas for improvement.

Financial enrolment in the vision

Enrolment can also come from financial incentives that lead to the team thinking like owners or shareholders rather than just employees. The financial rewards of ownership, whether big or small, go far beyond being paid for doing a job and deepen the employees' emotional connection and interest. Being an owner feels

---

4. M Watkins, *The First 90 Days, Updated and Expanded: Proven strategies for getting up to speed faster and smarter* (Harvard Business Review Press, 2013)

different from being an employee and it is this feeling of being part of something that accelerates growth. Because people feel part of something, their level of interest in it succeeding completely changes.

Equity ownership was a game-changer for us, and it's what led to our accelerated growth, especially during difficult times. I am a great believer in equity ownership for as many of the team as possible. The ways to achieve this are not always obvious, and the ownership can be small and still be effective. My experience was that a small equity stake that had been paid for outweighed a much larger option package in terms of motivation and the feeling of being part of something.

We reaped the benefits of having our team utterly enrolled in our vision when, just two weeks after our buyout in 2007 (where everyone went from employee to owner and employee), Northern Rock collapsed and the general financial crisis followed. Because our team was enrolled, thanks to the emotional connection and financial connection we had established, we were ready to weather the storm and do what needed to be done to grow. While our competitors lost clients, became despondent and stopped pitching for business, we took the opportunity to build market share and win clients. We accelerated our business plan throughout that downturn and went on to grow during every downturn since. Enrolment leads directly to growth. When you are all in it together, you grow faster.

Ownership through equity

You have to start thinking about equity ownership for your people in the early days, possibly when there's only you and you are about to recruit for the first time. An early decision you need to make is whether or not to make a potential future split of equity between you and your senior team, or those who might join your senior team. To attract good people who will fuel growth, you may need to offer them equity, so think about this from the start. Do you have space in the equity for your senior team, who are going to be important in driving growth? Who else might you need in the senior team over a long period, and what equity might you need to offer them? Are you prepared to have a co-founder? Are you prepared to have a key driver of the business to whom you're willing to give up equity? If you are, you need to manage that from the beginning.

Later, equity is a powerful tool to transform how people are enrolled in your vision. Part of enrolment is getting employees to think like owners or shareholders of the business, which changes what they are prepared to contribute towards its growth. The company's growth becomes a personal concern so that they are part of the growth journey, and share fully in the excitement and benefits of growth.

Getting a dividend cheque from your employer adds an emotional charge to your financial enrolment. It doesn't have to be a lot of money – you might only offer people £10 worth of shares – but it feels different, like a hit of serotonin. It's like growing a garden when you don't really know what will spring up. I used to buy something with my dividend cheques that I would otherwise never have spent money on because it felt different. My first dividend cheque was £2,000, and that money felt different to any other bonus I had ever received. I spent the whole dividend on a piece of art from the Affordable Art Fair, which still reminds me of what I set up and built. That is an emotional connection that salary and bonuses cannot replace.

Your team having an equity interest can enrol them in a way that nothing else can. This does not just have to be about what you give away, it can be used as a form of financing. So many businesses don't think of this route and don't include their team in discussions. You can even think about what your team can possibly contribute when you're looking for outside investment, as finnCap's own story shows. It always surprises me what people will do when given the opportunity.

Equity to supercharge enrolment

For finnCap, two big events drove the equity ownership of the business, and therefore how people viewed being equity holders and owners, and, as a result, how it affected their willingness to help drive growth.

When we first bought out the business from J M Finn (our parent company) in 2007, we had spent ten years growing the corporate finance and trading divisions within a much bigger business. The combined divisions were getting close to our £3m revenue target. We needed to invest £500k to set up a new division, which was our next route to growth, and this involved getting stock exchange approval to be an adviser to Alternative Investment Market quoted businesses. I needed to hire four key people who would get us our licence. If we wanted to grow, we had to make that investment.

Over the previous ten years, we had grown by reinvesting our own profits into our division, much like most start-ups. We reinvested our profits back into new hires, and growth was slow but consistent. Each year involved a relatively low-risk investment in new people, and we'd grown it with no equity incentive for us as individuals.

Accelerating growth from this point involved a much bigger and much higher-risk investment. We weren't prepared to put in our salaries to make this investment without an equity reward, which started the conversations about a buyout.

These conversations took a number of years and culminated in J M Finn agreeing that we could buy out our division and they would own 50% (50.01%, in fact) and our team the other 50%. It took me three years to negotiate that, because they started offering closer to 10% for the team with them owning 90%, which wasn't going to work. Once I finally had agreement on that

50%, we then needed to find that £500k to complete the MBO.

We would then have our own business, which would be called finnCap, and we would own 50% between the team. It was going to be about servicing small companies really well and having a different culture from everybody else in the space.

I had a spreadsheet to work out how the 50% was going to be split, and kept hiring on the promise of future equity. Importantly, it had to be fair. This spreadsheet must have changed multiple times a day over the seven months I had to complete the buyout, until I got it right, and not everyone will agree I got it right. When the final shareholdings were split, I started off with 9%. The key senior directors had 5%, many of them having taken a risk to join us with no certainty that the equity would be there. The more junior a person was, the less they got, but everybody had a fairly meaningful stake.

Various divisions were coming together under the finnCap banner: a sales team, a trading team and a corporate finance team – about twenty people altogether. Not everyone had got on brilliantly, and I thought my hardest job as CEO of the new company would be to get all the divisions working well together, cross-selling, liking each other and motivated by each other. I thought that getting everyone moving in the same direction would take me two years, and only then could we properly focus on growth.

The night before the buyout, we had a cheque-signing ceremony and everyone subscribed for their shares. I wrote a cheque for £90,000. The cheques added up to the £500k investment we needed to make. We had become owners. Overnight.

The next day, we came back to the same office, the same desks, as a collective. We were owners, not just employees, and everything had changed. We went from separate people running divisions, all reporting into the centre, all trying to do well for ourselves and the firm, to people who owned the whole business and had an interest in what everybody else was doing. It was just like everyone had been liberated. They were good, but they became great.

Everyone was willing to work with each other. They were willing to cross-sell. They were willing to drive the business in a different way. They were willing to put more effort in. They were willing to get to know people that maybe they wouldn't have known before. What I thought was going to be a two-year job turned out to be not a job at all. The bus was driving itself. Everyone having that equity ownership and writing meaningful cheques had overcome the growth challenges that I thought I might face in the early days. This was extremely lucky because, two weeks later, Northern Rock collapsed and we needed to be a coordinated, cohesive team.

We'd put up £500k of our own money and the market was going wrong. Northern Rock was opposite our office, so we could see how wrong it was going, and it got worse over the next two years as the general financial crisis took hold. Because we were all owners and enrolled, however, everybody was willing to go the extra mile. We took that downturn as an opportunity for growth because everybody was an owner. Rather than saying, 'We're going to have a bad year, I'm not going to get a bonus, I'm not going to work that hard and I'm depressed,' people said, 'Right, we're owning this, let's go. Let's take some market share while the market's bad.'

If we'd entered the financial crisis that followed the Northern Rock collapse with the wrong mindset, we might have gone under. Instead, we realised that we had an opportunity for growth because suddenly no one was servicing the companies we wanted as clients, and we could also hire people we could not have attracted before the downturn.

It was scary. My Head of Compliance and I were checking cash two or three times a day, maybe more, thinking: 'When is the point that we're going to all have to take a pay cut? When is the point that directors might have to stick their hands back in their pockets?' Every time, though, we'd get a bit more business that day – because we were trading shares, it was very live. Enrolment got us through. Each time the markets became difficult, we used that as a time to supercharge growth. That's all about already having the vision done, the excitement done, the enrolment done.

Because we had enrolled everyone in the vision with equity at the beginning, within four years, we were market leaders in our space with the largest number of AIM clients. We didn't look back until we reached £17m turnover. It was quite extraordinary how that equity ownership transformed what people were willing to do, in terms of helping other people, thinking about the bigger picture, striving towards a collective vision. Equity that leads to enrolment can save you two to three years in getting your team aligned, maybe even more.

Enrolment also means that the team will be willing to make sacrifices when needed. Once, the key leadership team took zero pay for three months, and a second time, when Covid hit, our entire team took a pay cut – the largest cut for the board and directors, then decreasing amounts so that the most junior took as small a cut as possible. We were all in it together. The enrolment as shareholders had made it much easier to make the sacrifices that were needed at the time they were needed.

The transformative power of equity ownership for all

Three years after our buyout, we had the opportunity to buy the remaining 50% owned by our parent company, J M Finn. This was my opportunity to make sure we took a different and much more inclusive approach to equity ownership, and for us, this was another game-changer. For this to work, everybody had to be given the option to get involved in equity if they wanted to. At the time of the buyout, I had got the parent company to agree to a 20% option pool, which meant J M Finn would get diluted below 50% over a period of time. I did this so that I would have shares to keep attracting talent as we moved forward.

After year three, though, we were running out of shares. We had been continually recruiting and I had used up the option pool. We still needed to recruit, but we didn't have any shareholding left without diluting everybody's existing shares. If we bought J M Finn out, we could have that shareholding to incentivise new people, who would buy shares out of the current valuation and be incentivised to grow it from there.

It took another year to negotiate how we could buy out that 50% for £2.5m (the market value of the parent company's shares). I knew that enrolment was of massive importance because of what had happened in finnCap's early days. How could we make this our real enrolment moment?

What I did next was transformational and potentially a bit risky. I decided to offer that 50% equally to every single person in the firm. There were now fifty of us, so everyone, from me to my PA, was offered the chance to buy £50,000 worth of shares. If anyone did not want to subscribe, or wanted to buy less, their £50,000 or part of it went back into the pot for others to buy if they wanted to. If anyone wanted more than £50,000 worth of shares, they had to put in an application to buy from the pot.

Doing this set out our stall from a cultural perspective and let everyone know that we were different. It made my team trust me in a way they didn't trust CEOs of our competitor firms, because they knew I would always look after them. It was risky because I wanted to keep my percentage the same and it could have been diluted. My chairman was nervous about the strategy, but I believed that this was our moment to be utterly fair, to enrol people not only in the equity, but also in the vision that we were a fair and inclusive business, that we were not like everybody else, where the top team takes it all and no one else gets anything. We wanted to be different.

Because the parent company didn't particularly want to sell the 50%, once they'd agreed I needed to move fast and I had a week to raise the £2.5m. I sat in a room, the employees came in one by one and I talked them through what we could do and told them up to £50,000 worth of shares could be available to them to buy. A representative from our bank, HSBC, was in the next room, offering personal loans secured on the shares depending on their personal circumstances. We committed to pay a dividend if we possibly could, so that that dividend income would pay any interest, to try to reduce the risk for people. Again, we were trying to make it as inclusive as possible. Everyone decided whether they went into the next room or not. I never knew if they did.

At the end of the week, everybody had to come back to me with their answer. I thought we might get £1m from the team, and I would have to raise the rest from third parties, so in that week I was also going around presenting to potential investors. Within forty-eight hours, I got almost £2.5m from my team. A couple of hundred thousand came from some outside shareholders, but over £2m came from me, my chairman, senior directors and the team. It was probably the proudest moment of my entire career. I was in tears as the cheques kept coming in. This was enrolment on a different level.

I still don't know, and will never know, who put their own money up, who borrowed from HSBC or who borrowed from their families. My PA ended up taking quite a good-sized shareholding, which was great. Some junior team members also took up quite big shareholdings. Not everyone could take up their £50,000 entitlement, but it was done in such a way that everyone had the option. What I always find astonishing is that, if I'd spread the equity in a more traditional way and said, 'I'm taking 10% of this and you can take the balance,' we would have ended up with exactly the same result. I ended up subscribing to get the shareholding I wanted.

It was a risky move, because if I'd ended up with all the senior people having the same equity as the juniors, that probably wouldn't have worked from an incentive point of view. It did work. We did get the right shareholdings. Everyone felt included.

The key takeaways from our story are:

- If you need to raise money, think first about going to your team.

- People having the chance to buy shares is important for enrolment, even if they choose not to buy them.

- The way we executed our second buyout not only escalated our growth, but set our inclusive culture and built trust in me as CEO when it was clear that I would not put myself above everybody else.

Incentives for growth need to align with your culture and vision as well as financial targets. Of course, not everyone can do what we did, but there are various ways you can help the team make a financial commitment in a way that aligns with your culture, including:

- An option package. You need to make sure to put good performance criteria around all the options. Stagger the vesting of the options so that everyone gets something valuable over time and you won't have periods of risk when there is no longer a share incentive. Set up something that will succeed, rather than something that will require your people to hit unrealistic targets – it's disheartening to expect a gain and then to miss it by a tiny margin. Having a range which scales with performance means that at least some options will be exercisable. If people lose all their options, the discussions can get surprisingly difficult.

- Asking people to invest their own money. You could suggest that they invest their bonus, or make it possible for them to put in a small amount. This is more effective in my experience than a big option package because the investment decision remains theirs and the dividend is something they have earned.

- Loaning employees the money to invest from the company's cash. This worked for us when we did it at finnCap in the early days because we could do it at scale and give people a decent holding.

- Save As You Earn (SAYE) schemes are often discounted because they're too small, or they cost a bit of money to put in place, or they are thought to be not worth it. If you want to get everybody at all salary levels enrolled in the equity, though, you need to think a bit more creatively. SAYE schemes are a great way to enrol junior members of staff in the equity, so that they can feel included.

We did two SAYE schemes, and both were effective at enrolment. The early-stage schemes are, obviously, much more effective because the growth can be exponential. As well as taking part in the two buyouts, our reception team and juniors could put a monthly amount of their salary – £10 or £20 – into buying equity. At the end of three years, they could choose to get the money back or buy the shares. Every month, they were buying £10 more equity, for a low price. Every time the company was doing better, they would know they'd made more money. Who knows whether this is the reason we have one of the best reception teams in the City, but I'd put my money on the fact that it had a large part to do with it. Giving away a small amount to everybody can be huge for enrolment, and then huge for growth.

The risks of not enrolling your people

If you don't start building that emotional connection as soon as your job offer has been accepted, it's hard to do it later. Your culture might have led your hire to accept, but you also need to keep reminding them, between offer and start, that they've made the right decision.

People are vulnerable to switching course at this point, even if they've signed a contract. Notice periods in your industry might be a minimum of three months, or longer for senior people. This is time in which your precious recruit's existing firm will try to coax them back, because no one wants to lose good people, or a bigger firm will hear that they're leaving and offer them more money.

This is where your culture can make it clear to your recruit, and anyone else wondering whether to work with you, that you do things differently from other firms, including where they work now and anywhere else they might consider joining.

Summary

Giving employees a sense of ownership through equity can be transformational, because your vision will then mean something personal to them and they will be enrolled both emotionally and financially. Asking someone to invest their own money (with support, if necessary) and giving them the chance to buy shares is more effective for enrolment than an option package. It's worth investing in schemes that mean the lower-paid staff can share in the company's success, because everyone is needed on board to supercharge growth. If the whole company can be enrolled together (as in the buyout described above), this will keep the team focusing on growth through the most challenging circumstances they face, because they will be performing as shareholders rather than employees.

SIX

Engagement: A Rich Mix

Introduction

Engagement is another way to think about inclusion. How do you make your people feel truly included on your growth journey and valued by your organisation, day to day, so that everyone is aligned? That feeling of belonging is what builds your team's engagement with your business, and it's achieved by building an open, inclusive culture in many small steps. If everyone is rowing in the same direction, the boat will move faster. Engaged teams that are aligned drive faster growth.

Businesses that are concerned about diversity need to work on engagement and inclusion first. We achieved diversity by working on inclusion. If you have an inclusive culture, you will attract talented people who want to work for you and recommend you to their friends and colleagues. Inclusive cultures help you see blind spots, identify growth opportunities, and stop 'groupthink'. Growth quite often comes from doing things differently, so different perspectives matter.

People will go above and beyond for a good culture where they're connected and engaged. If they're engaged, they're involved in growth, they're committed, and they'll come up with ideas to grow more. The culture of engagement, the culture of inclusion, is a culture that scales: it leads to growth because everyone is part of it.

Little things make a big difference

Small gestures that make people feel valued and important make a big difference to engagement. People love their efforts to be seen and acknowledged, and small monetary and non-monetary rewards can do a lot to build and sustain engagement.

As well as regular bonuses, we had a pot of exceptional bonuses for special achievements. If someone was doing something especially good, above and beyond their job, we would give them a small, one-off bonus that wasn't expected. I'd write them a personal letter setting out what they had done and why it was so valuable, and I'd give them the letter personally. They wouldn't be expecting it, they would be delighted, and it would mean more than a much larger bonus that they had been expecting. These one-off bonuses could range from

£100 to £10,000 for something exceptional, but people valued the reassurance of being seen and recognised more than the amount, and they would invariably give even more in return. We used to give all the team who completed a deal over a certain large figure a special present, which also made people feel valued.

There are many non-monetary gestures that need to be tailored to the individual that will make them feel that they matter. You might let them know that you've noticed they have worked particularly hard, perhaps giving them an extra day off. Or you might have a good one-to-one talk where you ask questions like, 'Are you the best version of yourself? How can we get you there?' Questions like this can help you understand an individual's drive and motivation, which will be different for everyone. Notice when people are struggling, give support or time out when needed, and offer to help with solutions to their problems. These small, thoughtful things do take time and effort, but they matter in bringing to life a culture in which people feel truly valued.

Plus, you need to use your regular structures to best effect: do reviews that make a difference to people, work out where they need to go, accelerating them as fast as you possibly can (see Chapter 8) and giving them the training and support they need. I am a massive fan of coaching, so we got a lot of people one-to-one coaches to help them on their journeys. This was seen to add a lot of value.

Once you've set out your intention to be a great place to work and are noticing the difference, get publicly recognised for it. This recognition will ensure that good corporate culture stays prominent, and a priority. There are a number of lists that identify the really great places to work, such as Great Place to Work® and Best Workplaces™. I always found that making it a goal to be on one of these lists was worth the time spent due to the benefits of good PR and brand recognition, which really drive engagement. Employees love hearing their company talked about in a good way.

Everyone contributes to the whole

At finnCap, we consistently took every opportunity to bring everyone into the fold and involve them in key moments and milestones on our growth journey.

- When we needed to formally set our values, we took a collaborative approach, bringing in consultants to work with the whole team (then around twenty-five people) in small groups of six to eight people. We asked everyone to write down what was special about finnCap. They needed to be taken on by everyone, and it wouldn't have worked for me, as CEO, to write down the values and say, 'Here you go.'

- We went through the same process twice in ten years. At first, we set five values, then when we grew to sixty or seventy people, we distilled the five into three (smart-thinking, dynamic and collegiate), and used a similar process to work on our mission, with everyone having a chance to feed in in the same way.

- Before both our office moves, we took groups to see the shortlisted choices and talked through their concerns or ideas about the new space. We showed people various designs and branding options. For the first new office, we had a vote on what to put in the spare space; a table tennis table got the top vote!

- We made sure everyone could come to town hall meetings. The receptionists were asked to leave the reception desk and make sure they could hear what was being said.

Including everyone in the firm on your growth journey means not only including your key revenue generators, but also the people who are driving the systems that enable you to get revenue, such as reception, IT, operations. There's a real benefit to making sure that everyone understands everyone else's role, and that everyone knows how their function is relevant to the big picture and why they make a difference. This gets everyone wanting to go in the same direction.

INCLUDED AND UNIQUELY VALUED FROM THE START

Engagement starts on day one. The earlier you build engagement in a new team member, the easier it will be. We have established that the first ninety days after a new person joins are critical, especially if they are a senior person who might shift the dynamic of the business. This period is a one-off opportunity to maximise the new person's engagement with you, and to make them engaged with everybody else. After ninety days, it is harder to have the same impact.

As outlined in the previous chapter on enrolment, we put time and effort into an extremely detailed ninety-day plan for everyone, and that hard work paid off by making them feel engaged.

Where do you get your ideas from? Everywhere!

People who are engaged will generate ideas, as long as you have created a good environment for ideas to be generated. If people feel their ideas are truly welcome and will be properly considered, they will be more engaged. As previously stated, don't forget to include back-office staff. We had phenomenal ideas from our reception team, whom I introduced in Chapter 4, and our IT department brought ideas for serving the team better so the team could serve clients better.

You need everyone to have ideas for growth because, as the CEO, you cannot have all the ideas you need. A junior member of staff can have just as good ideas as you. The tiny ideas can be the most useful ones. Twenty small tweaks are worth more than one big idea. You need a culture in which people are able to talk, share thinking and feedback that will encourage people to say, 'That process is a bit rubbish. We can speed that up. Why don't we try...'

With help from a brilliant intern from the Centre for Entrepreneurs, we worked on how to create ideas and bring them into the business effectively. After some awaydays working on how to get people to participate, we set up a smart-thinking platform – a virtual suggestion box where people could send in their ideas anonymously. If you create an environment in which people can get involved, and they see something happening as a result, or there's feedback to them but they have not been outed in the process, you create more trust and openness.

The ideas could be questions. Why are we using that form? Why are we using that paper? Why are we doing that? Does the client like that? Or they could be concerns from which consistent themes emerged that we could address at a town hall.

The premise was to create growth in revenue or profit, or both, by lots of people making small incremental changes, or lots of small incremental changes added together by the same team. Growth doesn't have to come from one ground-breaking idea. It can come from constantly tweaking processes to make them a bit more efficient, or cost a bit less, or give clients a slightly better service. As in the principle of compound interest, tiny tweaks over time suddenly make a big difference.

You could take market share just by ensuring that everyone is constantly thinking about what could change and what could improve. You might not grow as fast as the person who has also got new ideas and is in a big growth sector, but there will always be something that can be done better or more efficiently.

GET AWAY TO GET MORE ENGAGEMENT

As your team expands, finding the time and space to get everyone together becomes more difficult. Awaydays for the whole team are logistically difficult (especially when you can't get everyone together at the same time), they cost money and they take a long time to plan and organise. They are also a potential HR headache. That said, I never found anything that engaged people in the same way as actually getting away from the office. Going abroad for at least a day and a night would be even better for generating ideas, improving communication and getting overall better results.

We tried to take groups of around twenty or thirty people away every two years, making sure that teams were split to encourage as much cross-company communication and understanding as possible. This always resulted not only in excellent ideas to keep the business growing and a reinvigorated team, but, most importantly, a team that knew each other better than before. They had some downtime getting to know each other, they had fun, and they participated in some well-crafted team-building sessions and strategy and ideas sessions to ensure it was as valuable as possible. The awaydays became a real highlight for the team and something to look forward to. We would get as many people as possible involved and engaged in the planning, and we would always follow up on their ideas for future awaydays.

New teams bring more ideas

Every time you acquire a business or recruit a new person or new team, you get another source of new ideas that you would not have otherwise had. One of the reasons I thought our new CEO, who first joined us through acquisition, was the right person for the job was that, in his previous head of department role, he had been looking at using technology to work differently and save money. When there was a talent drain and we couldn't employ new people, he used a company that did corporate finance with an outsourcing model. They could do different things at different times; you could add a person, you could take off a person, and you didn't have to pay those people a bonus or bring them in equity. You could pay the existing team more by outsourcing some of the junior work to this different way of working. That was a big idea that I would never have had, from a new management team who we had successfully engaged, and created a good saving for the business.

The feedback loop

Listening is important if you are to create a good corporate culture, but listening and hearing are two different things, and people need to be listened to and heard. The effect of having an open culture is that people feel included in conversations and feel heard when they give feedback, answer survey questions and make suggestions. What many companies are missing, is a way to deal with the answers and the suggestions in a way that makes people feel heard.

There is a range of ways to gather employees' feedback: surveys, one-to-ones, asking good questions. As discussed in Chapter 3, people's communication styles vary enormously, so communicating in a range of ways and testing their relative effectiveness is important when working on engagement.

We appointed two upcoming leaders to run employee forums (one for levels up to assistant director and one for more senior levels) and gave them a budget. They had a direct line to me, as CEO, which made them feel part of the company. The forums themselves were a way for us to find out, without management being involved, how we were doing at making people feel included.

In the feedback loop, you ask for employees' feedback, listen to their points, reflect on the information and – crucially – go back and tell people what you have done with their input. You do this even if you are not able to act on their input, or not for the moment. You need to feed back on the many ideas you will gather, some of which won't work. Even if you tell people their idea does not work, or you can't make it a priority at the moment, the evidence that you have listened and considered it makes them feel that they haven't been ignored; that their idea or their piece of feedback hasn't vanished into the ether. It's disheartening to give feedback and have no response.

You can do group feedback along the lines of: 'We've had some great ideas for this, and these are the ones we are taking forward and this is why a few of them didn't work'. If you share as much of your thinking as you can, people will know that you listened to their ideas and you've got a reason for your response.

Every April, when we launched the next year's goals and KPIs, we included ideas that we had gathered from the whole company. We started in January, getting individual teams to have sessions and feed up ideas for the management strategy session. They could make suggestions for the whole company as well as their own department. When we launched the strategy at a town hall, people would know that some of their ideas would be included and we would acknowledge other ideas, while, with the feedback loop in mind, explaining that we weren't ready for them yet.

Benefits of inclusive budget setting

Budget setting is a key annual process that becomes more relevant as you get bigger, and extremely relevant if you are a listed business or have a venture capital or private equity backer. Budget and forecasting need to be well thought through, and also seen as another opportunity to foster engagement.

If the whole team is involved in setting the budget, the likelihood of hitting it increases hugely. We got the various teams to do bottom-up budgets for the service lines, as well as sector teams looking along sector lines. We then looked at a top-down view of our competitors and the market as a whole, and came up with what we thought was sensible. The targets mean more when the teams have had a say in setting them, and this also gives them responsibility. Growth targets can then be matched to the right incentives so that everyone is aligned and you maximise your chances of achieving them.

Managing for engagement

As you scale, you can't personally work on engaging everyone and fully understand every individual's motivation. You need managers to do this for you. Anyone who is managing people needs to be real, open, authentic and consistent, because that is what builds trust and empowers people to do their best.

Managers are typically not trained to look beyond their own idea of what a hard-working team member ought to look like. If a team member seems unproductive, they are not necessarily disengaged. Their colleagues (or their manager) might be annoying them, or their pet might have just died and they are out of sorts. They might even be distracted for a positive reason: perhaps they've had a brilliant idea which is absorbing their attention. People have a lot going on behind the scenes, and if they seem unfocused, finding out why has massive benefits and builds trust.

Across a team, there will be a wide range of motivations to manage – or there should be, because a team should ideally include a range of personality types. In addition, levels of confidence and insecurity will vary widely between individuals and need to be taken into account. Managers have to be trained to be aware that a team member will not necessarily react as they would react to any event or circumstance.

We found the World Class Manager programme helpful here, to train managers to fully understand their role.

This included training them to respond with empathy and kindness to people having a bad day, having family problems, about to go off on maternity leave, or any other circumstance that needs understanding.

Engagement for management

While you rely on managers to foster engagement, how do you make sure managers themselves are engaged with the vision? Are you sharing strategy with them? Can they feed into the strategy and how does that feed up to the top?

How you communicate with your key management team will change as you scale. At first, you might have a weekly update with all your managers, but as you grow, you have to have another level of management and you might not meet with those people so frequently. As finnCap grew, the shape of our management team constantly changed. As you expand, you need to keep finding ways to keep people feeling part of the journey, and it's not easy, because it's just not possible for everyone to have a say in everything. You keep asking: what works in meetings? What do people want to talk about?

If you build a new division, or acquire a division from another company, you need to consider how to make it part of your management structure and make everyone feel included. When you buy in a team, you will usually decide who is going to be running it: can they represent that team in the management structure? Does every new division get a seat at the top table? When we had fifteen people on the top team, we realised it was slightly too big, so we had to shrink the top tier back and still make people feel included.

To do this, we ended up with a small group of six leaders in the key top roles, with groups below them managing the various divisions and feeding up. We started a business leaders' group for all the senior leaders, focusing on how to communicate strategy. While they weren't immediately involved in weekly decision-making, they were in a direct relationship with it.

Dealing with a lack of engagement

Lack of engagement is more long term than lack of excitement, and more likely to be a problem. People can be engaged without being super-excited, though lack of excitement can be an early warning sign of lack of engagement, so you need to be alert to it. Non-engagement can move from something that sounds passive to something quite disruptive. People who are not engaged are picking up the phone to a headhunter, they're not turning up to things, they're starting to think more negatively about the company.

You can sometimes spot non-engagement at town halls or group meetings, when people are looking out of the window, but you are more likely to get an early warning if you're present in the office and chatting to people, noticing if anyone doesn't seem to feel part of things. It's not always about who doesn't volunteer for something or doesn't seem keen; that might be disengagement with the process rather than the company. The next chapter also discusses how to pick up these signals.

If you talk to people regularly and ask good questions, you can find out what makes them happy and what might become a problem before they become disengaged. If you check that they are aware of their strengths and weaknesses, you can help them play to their strengths.

Listening is also a valuable tool. You can learn a huge amount from being in meetings and doing a lot more listening than talking. Notice who is quiet, who wants to say something but can't, learn what excites and annoys individuals. Listening can be one of the best tools for improving your performance as a CEO.

Some people are fully engaged as you grow because growth excites them, and they want to grow, too. Others might not like change, and might be less engaged five years in, and perhaps feel slightly less relevant as you scale. Is there a way you can make them feel part of things, perhaps by changing their role or title, if not keeping them in the seat they were in before?

If someone seems not to be working at full power, or perhaps a few people, it's easy to get annoyed, but I usually found it helpful to reflect on whether I had found out what their driver was, what motivated them and what else might be going on in their life. Motivation is personal to the individual, so your employees are not going to automatically share your motivation. You have to do the work to understand each individual on a deeper level, or train your managers to do it so that they get beyond simply saying, 'That person is not working hard today.'

Disengagement with the company can be related to someone's concerns about the direction their career is going in, or fear that a manager who they don't like will never leave. It might be a time in their life when all their friends are getting promotions and pay rises but they're not. You won't know any of this unless you spend the time and effort having those conversations.

Some people will tell you that they're not engaged if you ask them directly (although women are less likely to do this), so they might reveal a reason that you can address, like a lack of career progression or feeling that they're not in the loop, or you might learn something you didn't know about them.

The more you and your managers can understand each individual and make them feel valued, the closer to the best version of themselves they will be, the less you will need to manage them in future, and the less likely it is that you will need to lose them. If you do, conduct detailed exit interviews (see Chapter 9). Try to work out the point at which the person became disengaged and whether you could have made a difference. If their lack of engagement is because they don't like your business or your strategy, perhaps you can't do anything about it, but the sooner you find out the better.

Summary

You have to invest time and money in your end goal of making everyone feel valued and helping them maximise their potential, which includes training managers to be empathetic. You have to have many conversations, which are, of course, time-consuming for you as the leader and easy to put aside when you have a lot going on. Think, though, of the emotional cost of managing people out and the financial cost of recruiting to replace them, and a little effort starts to seem like a much better deal.

If you have an engaged team and you create a great place to work, they will give your growth journey their all and make it fun. Your holy grail is for everyone to be the best version of themselves. If you can achieve that, then you will be in a great place and you're likely to grow fast.

SEVEN

Energy: Shelf Life

The long-term value of happiness for growth

Energy drives engagement, smart thinking, ideas and growth. Energy is what sustains performance, and creating energy is your job as CEO. It is exhausting and relentless and it needs your focus to sustain a regular buzz. As you scale, senior leaders and managers will be responsible for creating this energy within their teams and this will need a process and training. The ability to generate energy is an important factor to consider in promoting and hiring your senior team.

I also think of energy as a 'fizz factor' that can super-charge your growth. During periods in which you're doing well, the market's good and you're winning, you'll find the energy easily. You'll be in that zone where there is real momentum and buzz, and you've got to take advantage of it. At other times, when the market's not with you, you're in recession, you're not winning clients, you will need to turn up the fizz factor and generate your own energy. When finnCap's growth plateaued at around £17m, we needed to find a way to re-energise because the market wasn't growing. That meant sharing a new mission to get people excited again.

Energy is created by making your company a great place to work, where everyone is valued, and this was our focus from the start. We stood out from our competitors for our commitment to caring about our team, valuing them, and for having fun when the general focus of the financial services sector was making money, with valuing people and having fun coming second. It works the other way round. If your people are valued and have fun at work and your team is happy, you will make money. Possibly more money than those with miserable employees.

You are the energy source

As CEO, you are responsible for the daily energy of the business (or mood music, as one of my executive board used to say). It is this energy that makes people want to come to work, so that they feel good on a Sunday night because they are going to work on Monday. A happy and thriving workforce is productive. If people want to be at work – in a great environment where they can excel, come up with ideas, go the extra mile, have fun – that will drive productivity and therefore drive growth.

Maintaining energy in the long term, which keeps morale high, has a different quality to generating the energy and excitement that led people to buy into and share your vision. You no longer have that first buzz of something brand new, but you still have to keep people motivated and moving forward. Energy comes and goes quickly, and you have to sense when it's dipping – perhaps during difficult times or when you've lost a client – and be able to bring it back up.

Generating energy is tiring, and it needs to be done even when you're having a bad day. In fact, you cannot be seen to be having a bad day. Whatever is going on in the background, you have to be like a swan – legs flapping like mad invisibly underwater, but above the surface, all must be effortlessly calm, controlled, positive and open. This takes its toll, especially when things are going wrong or markets are bad.

As you grow, you might find ways to get help with creating the energy, but you can't ever let go of it completely or hand it over to HR. It's an area where you will always have to stay on the front foot if you want to grow.

Checking the energy pulse

How do you give your team energy? How are you monitoring the combined energy of the whole team? First, you've got to be actively concerned about it. It should be on your agenda (literally, an item on the agenda at management team meetings so that it is talked about) and a visible priority.

What doesn't get measured doesn't get done, so you need your own reliable sense of what state the business's energy is in without needing to do an employee survey. It might be that having a good sense of this isn't in your skill set, though I've always found it an important part of my role. Nonetheless, keep energy levels on your radar or you're likely to forget about it, and consider where you can get help with pulse checking. Who in your organisation is good at listening to people and hearing what is going on? You need to know who those people are and make sure you check in with them regularly.

In my early days, my PA was involved in all sorts of things within the business, so she was connected to everybody and had great, down-to-earth relationships with the team. One of the key roles she had, on a confidential basis, was to tell me where the energy was dipping and where I might need to spend some time. You might find the head of HR, the head of marketing, the head of operations or someone in your top team is good at this. It needs to be someone with high emotional intelligence, to whom people feel they can go with a problem.

As we grew, we appointed specific members of staff who were good at connecting with people to lead our staff forums. The forum leaders would feed back confidentially to the management team and me on the team's general attitude about various issues, but in the early days, you just need your own process for finding out what's going on.

I started by focusing on key questions which, I had read, gave a good indicator of a team's happiness and therefore their productivity. When I first realised that culture was key to growth, it was a relatively new concept without a lot of previous thinking to draw on. I needed to research the right mix of questions (not too many of them, fewer than ten). One of the questions I used to get a good indication of overall well-being at work was, 'Do you have a good friend at work?' It turned out we were pretty good at that. In our early days, one of the team pointed out that people looked forward to Monday mornings because they saw their friends. We had breakfast for everyone and people joked around. Our Sunday nights did feel good.

As we grew, and the number of employees rose, the questions had to change. You can now buy in or commission all sorts of staff pulse-checking surveys, so that aspect of the CEO role is much easier. However, I found that being personally involved in this process and giving focused thought about which questions to ask was worth the time.

Celebrate and connect for the buzz

How can you add the 'fun factor' and get people together socially? It can take some thought and effort, but there's always something. It can be hard work to keep bringing people together for downtime when you're busy, but it's relatively straightforward and can simply mean having a night out or a bonding session.

When we came back after Covid and people were spending different days in the office, we started having group lunches on Wednesdays so that everyone could be together on at least one day and have a free lunch. The team would sit and chat, sometimes only for a short time, but this made a real difference and enabled people to connect with one another.

It's not essential to meet up in person to connect. At this same time, we also started a 'Friday Feeling' email round-up, detailing everything positive that was going on in the company: good news or nice comments from customers. I always found small things to celebrate, details about individuals' achievements that were inspiring to share. The reception team would send a weekly quiz or a challenge to guess lines from films. Our Investor Relations team would always ask a few funny questions at the end of emails. These small, thoughtful efforts to add some fun to communications created a real feeling of energy. Encourage as many of these contributions as you can – the more the merrier. It does build a special connection.

After every deal, the deal leader would send out a message talking about it – who was involved and why it was important, creating a buzz about it. It was funny, personal and always different, because it was written in the style of the person sending it. When someone worked on their first successful deal after joining us, we would celebrate. As well as a shout out, they would often get a surprise present sent to their home, which really did create energy. Or perhaps someone would do something fantastic outside work, like complete a great charitable bike ride, or a triathlon or a big fundraiser. We always made a fuss of these achievements.

People respond well to constant praise, to being noticed and having good behaviours and every small success celebrated. A short email from the CEO that notices and comments on an achievement is extremely powerful.

Energy for tough times

Sometimes, it might feel hard to celebrate. There might be a recession, or you might have lost clients that week. The kind of problems in the market that make people uneasy can come from many external sources. We felt the effects on our energy from the Northern Rock collapse (weeks after our MBO), the general financial crisis that followed, Brexit, the war in Ukraine and the 2022 mini budget. When upheavals like this happen, you need to act fast to reassure the team and stop energy plummeting, and it can be hard. You might have to present the vision and mission again in a different way, or even change the mission.

Consistent communication is even more important during these energy slumps. You need to tell people how you are going to get through the difficult times and reiterate the big picture. If you sense that everyone is feeling a bit low, you might have to have more regular meetings, have an extra town hall, or return to the vision every day. There are endless ways to raise spirits and the smallest things can be effective – emails, visuals, videos, using comedy in messaging, informal meet-ups, group catch-ups, the list goes on – but it all needs thought and can easily become a low priority when it feels like there is a crisis to manage.

Sometimes, if everyone is in a bad mood, it might be that you just need to get them all in a room and let them vent and talk about what's going wrong. You may not be able to solve all the problems, but you can at least address the issues and let everyone know they have been heard.

During Covid, when motivation was particularly low, we would call people personally on a regular basis to check they were alright. We held regular town halls online and sent regular messages about our strategy and how we were still going to grow in the medium term. We acknowledged that the next six months were going to be a bit tricky, but we made sure everyone knew that we were all there and we were going to get through it as a team.

When you're in the middle of a difficult period, while thinking about how you're going to get through it, you've got to plan for how you're going to get people back to their full energy. You have to do this because you can't personally give everyone energy, all day, every day. Even if you have a culture of keeping energy high, there are always going to be pockets within teams and individuals whose energy is typically low. You always need to be conscious of whose energy is down, and plan for how you will get their energy back up.

The energy pyramid

Once you start growing beyond thirty or forty people, you will have to rely on your management structure to create some of the energy. People don't get management skills from thin air; you have to train them. They might have been good at their job when they became a manager, and not needed much training before. They might not realise that a manager's job isn't just to hit a budget and run a team – it's also about creating the energy that empowers the team. The World Class Manager programme that we used was great at getting managers to realise that they were responsible for energy, but you will probably have to show them how to do it and energise them so that they can energise their teams.

Some people are naturally high energy, and motivational, but it is harder to find them below exec team level. At lower management levels, there might be quite a mixture of energies. As you grow, it's important to hire and promote people with energy or who are good at generating it, because they will understand how to create energy and will have it on the agenda. That was certainly one reason why I always tried to promote from within. If your managers are working towards the same energy agenda, you personally won't have to create so much of it. Of course, you still need to manage your managers to keep the energy consistent, and I found that that was the hardest job as we scaled.

If one of your managers is having a problem or a difficult life event, and therefore their whole team have low energy, how do you help them? How do you get them to see the problem, to get some coaching? This is likely to happen many, many times a year in different departments, especially as you're growing, when there will be a lot of changes in the structure of your departments and a lot being asked of managers.

When the energy dips

You have to be good at not only spotting shifts in group energy, but also when individuals or teams have been under exceptional pressure. You can see what has happened in the NHS, post Covid. At the time of writing, in 2023, the workforce is on its knees and nothing has been done to re-energise them after what they've been through.

You can sometimes detect energy dips by tracking your teams' KPIs. You might also discover through an employee survey, or from one of your pulse checkers, that the energy in a particular team is not great. If you're not actually with the team, or you have outsourced your IT or other back-office departments, how can you make sure that those out-of-sight teams are happy? How do you spot if their managers are not performing? There will be ways you can find out, but you need to keep that team on your radar.

Then, if a problem shows up, you can take the manager aside and ask, 'What's happening? What can we do?' There might be a simple solution: that the team has been working unbelievable hours; that everyone is tired; or, in a more extreme case, they're burnt out with no energy left – but you still need to perform for your client. What can you do to help those people? Give the manager a budget to take them out. Give them a break. Give them some extra time off.

If an individual team member is performing poorly, the first task, as discussed in Chapter 6, is to find out why. They might not have been set the right goals, they may be having a bad week, or they may just need a day off to go and catch up on something in their personal life. Sometimes, it's a case of giving someone a pep talk, making sure they feel valued, or they might need a longer break, in which case you can send them on a holiday. In the worst cases, they may need extended time off.

You've got to address performance problems early. If you don't have a system to make you aware of issues, by the time you know about them, it may be too late and you end up in an exit process.

Quality conversations

A key takeaway from the World Class Manager programme, for us, was the importance of good-quality conversations, when you are sitting down with one of your team and asking, 'How are you? What's going on?' Just a chat, with no agenda. Keep it separate from any talk about performance, where people feel pressure to explain why they didn't perform well in a certain area and give a million excuses, or prove how well they did something else. I've never asked any of my team, 'How are you?', and not ended up in a quite long and useful conversation. It is amazing how people open up when you ask the question and are interested in the answer.

You need to make sure your managers are having these open, one-to-one chats with their teams, separate from any performance review, once every quarter or half year. Quite often, people are much more likely to share issues with their manager than with you, the CEO. They might be open with you, but they're much more likely to be open with someone just a little bit above them.

If those quality conversations happen at team level, and they're fed back up, you'll start understanding where the energy problems are and can help your managers work out what to do about it. There isn't a cookie-cutter approach to this, and you can't give the manager a manual for it. Ideally, you will be appointing managers with high EQ (emotional quotient) or who are willing to work on their EQ. You need to make looking after their teams a priority for your managers, and tie it into their compensation structure. You might have a great manager who gets the team to perform, but who may not spend any time looking after his people. If you have too many managers like that, you're not going to grow.

Quality moments

There are many significant corporate events that can be of great benefit in energising your team. Completing big fundraising rounds, IPOs, acquisitions and exits (where teams have a new owner to continue the growth path) can all be hugely energising, if managed well.

They can accelerate growth plans, energise the team to the next level, and create real excitement.

They can also cause a lot of uncertainty and concern if not managed well. When planning these events, it's crucial to consider their implications for the team, the messages you'll send about them and the timing of these messages. Most of the details of a transaction (whether an exit, IPO or fundraiser) will be highly confidential until near the end of negotiations, or, most likely, right up until the day they are announced. They might come as a big surprise and will raise many questions from the existing team and, if an acquisition, from a new team as well.

It is important to be well prepared for these questions and to think not only about how to communicate the right messages, but also how to use this significant moment to build energy and excitement. Most of these transactions will supercharge growth to the next level, so in order to get good buy-in to the new vision, it is important to explain clearly why the transaction has happened, how it relates to the team, and why it is in the team's interests. Explain who your great new shareholder is, for example, and what they can do for the company, or how an IPO might monetise staff shareholdings, or how an exit may mean the company will be taken to the next stage of growth with a new and exciting owner. Giving as much detail as you can, as soon as you can, and focusing on all the positives, will create good energy. The announcement must be planned and ready to go as soon as the transaction is live – if your team hears it through the grapevine or feels like they were the last people to know, it will create real culture problems and destroy trust.

DRAWING ENERGY FROM AN IPO

When finnCap completed its IPO in December 2018, it was an exciting time, especially given that a large number of the team were shareholders. This was a real moment for everyone to get energised and we made the most of the opportunity to set ourselves on the path to our next stage of growth. We started the day of our IPO with a reception for the whole team at 7.30am, followed by the opening of the London Stock Exchange at 8am, where we had photographs and speeches. It was a big celebration; everyone was involved and everyone had a chance to be proud of their achievements.

How are you, really?

To keep yourself as the energy carrier for the whole company, you must treat yourself like a super athlete. If you have a bad day, everybody is going to know about it. Sustaining the level of energy you need is only possible by giving yourself a brain break when you need one, in whatever form works for you.

Give yourself the support you need, get a coach to help you manage yourself through the process. Remember that if your head goes down, everyone else's does, too.

Summary

Sustaining growth needs a consistent level of positive energy in the business, and a blast of energy at the right time can supercharge your growth. The energy levels within your organisation need to be constantly on your radar, and you need a process for checking them so that the much-needed fizz factor can be boosted when necessary, and recovering from energy dips and external challenges can be quick.

It's not sustainable for you to personally generate enough energy for the whole business, so you will need to hire and promote with energy in mind and train your managers to be energy carriers. You need to build opportunities for energy boosts into your culture, and if you have successfully created a culture that scales, these opportunities will keep appearing.

EIGHT

Elevation: Extra Spice

Invest in your future leaders

Elevation is about how you can use the culture of your business as you scale to retain and empower the people who are going to deliver your vision, while at the same time developing your next generation of leaders. If you've done your work on Engagement, you will know how to make your people feel utterly and uniquely valued, and help them be the best versions of themselves they can be. If you can build on this approach to find and nurture your next top team, you will bring depth and sustainability into your business.

People are your key assets, and it is largely people who are going to drive your growth. I have always found that the best way to ensure a culturally aligned team is to find great talent at the early stages of their career and grow with them, so they one day become your 'culture carriers' and senior leadership team. They have been moulded into exactly how you want your team to be: how they treat people absolutely aligns with your culture, their energy is exactly what you need, and their understanding of your vision and core values is deep. Nurturing talent takes time, but it is worth it and it can save you from having to make key hires later, which can be expensive, with senior people difficult to attract and not as culturally aligned.

Growing your team requires time and planning. It means having a talent-acquisition strategy, and it means having a great review process and check-in system to ensure you know where everyone wants to go. Above all, it means making sure everyone in your team knows that you believe they are capable of quick career progression.

I have always believed in promoting people as soon as possible. If someone shows a skill set capable of moving up, I have sometimes even promoted them before they are quite ready, but knowing that the opportunity will be appreciated and that, with extra help, they will make it.

Investing in your future leaders is just that: an investment. It is your succession plan, your driver of new ideas, your cultural glue and your continuity. HR can help with this, but there is nothing that makes someone feel like a future leader better than *you*, as the CEO, spending time with them. It is worth the effort.

How to invest in your future leaders

One of the skillsets I used most as a leader was strong emotional intelligence, dealing with people and working out who is going to fit best in which roles in the future, and how to get them there. You might not have that skillset now, but you can build it by spending time with people, properly empathising and understanding their motivation, and not assuming they will react in the same way as you. Train your managers to develop these skills, too, and to do meaningful appraisals. Promote people into management who have emotional intelligence or good potential to develop it.

One of my breakthrough moments in the early days, after reading many books about leadership and psychology, was realising that everyone has their own way of thinking about things. Assuming that someone feels the same way as you, about exactly the same event, is not going to work. As I outlined in Chapter 6, you have to get to know the person if you're to work out what makes them tick, what drives them and what motivates them. Everyone is unique in that respect, and I have never found two people who thought in an identical way. Once I realised this, I allocated time to properly getting to know my team members and connecting with them as individuals, which helped them feel valued by the company. People who are valued go the extra mile.

This involves a lot of work, albeit work that I enjoy. If you are really not attracted to this kind of activity, it is possible to delegate some of it, and there are now senior roles with titles like Chief of Staff, Head of Culture or Head of People, but you will have to have grown a lot to justify such an appointment, and long before that – right from the beginning, once you have committed to growth – you will need to know where your future leaders are coming from and understand them as well as you can.

Your non-perishable store of superstars

In a fast-growing business, you are constantly making shifts in your leadership team and repositioning people. You need to be aware of who you will need in key roles in five or ten years' time. You can't rely on bringing the right people in when you need them. You need a full store of potential leaders who have embraced your culture which you can tap into when you need them for crucial roles, while ensuring that they are energised and motivated along the way, not waiting on a dusty shelf for their moment to shine. This means thinking ahead about where your next generation are, growing them into the roles you have in mind for them, and choosing the right moment to elevate them.

As you scale, you need to know who in the team is going to carry your culture forward, and you need to make sure that you have enough of these people at each level. Who is going to be each level's culture champion? Junior employees are extremely relevant here, because they can be the 'culture carriers' for their cohort and you can accelerate them into the teams that need them.

Once you know who your rising stars are, it's important that you show them your big picture and make sure they know how you see their acceleration through the business. Don't assume they know if you don't tell them. That means making sure you are proactive in having conversations in which you say, 'You're great at this. What are you thinking about your career progression?' If you can make it clear to people when they are fairly junior where you think they could go, that you believe in them and that you will help them get there, this will tie them in and build their loyalty.

Managing promotions

Once you have identified your future leaders and helped them get ready for their next role, they will, at some point, be promoted. This process needs careful management or you risk undoing a lot of good work, possibly alienating and losing other key people, or changing your culture.

It is important to prepare others for a potential promotion as well as the person being promoted, spending time on one-to-one discussions beforehand. This is especially important when it is a peer who is being promoted. Use these conversations to check what people might think of that person in a leadership role. Some people will be jealous, some won't like the idea of a new boss, some might think you have made a mistake. They will have all these feelings even more acutely if the appointment takes them by surprise, so prepare them well.

When a person takes over their new role, you need to make sure the elevation works. Preparing them for what the role entails and a period of careful shadowing is critical. You don't want the person who you have just elevated to fail, and they will need support. Again, the first ninety days are important, so you need to make a detailed ninety-day action plan for them once they are announced in their new position.

In the best promotions I have made, the individuals did an excellent job, but all needed help in the early days. A new role is hard, especially when it involves leading a team, and I always tried to persuade new leaders to use an external coach as well as spending time with them myself to ensure a successful transition into their new role.

You cannot do what many leaders do: think the work of elevation is done as soon as you have announced the promotion. It is only done when the team accepts and respects the person in their new role, and they are doing the job well. Until then, the elevation is a work in progress. A lot of people think they can manage and lead a team, but most can't. If you do make a mistake and the promotion is not working, you may need to make an urgent intervention to make it work quickly, or take some other action. Having the wrong leader in place is an absolute growth blocker.

Growing your top team

When you make your first senior hires, you are likely to be between £500k and £3m revenue, because, when you get to £500k, or even £1m, it's hard to do everything yourself – you certainly can't get to £3m without a proper team, albeit a small one, and without being willing to delegate. At just over £1m turnover, finnCap were five people, and by £3m, when we did our buyout, we were around twenty.

Ideally, when you start hiring you'll do so with a view to people staying with you far into the future. As well as asking if they have the right skills, you ask yourself, 'Is this person aligned? Do I trust them? Can I work with them?' You have to resist the temptation to hire someone or promote someone because a job needs doing and you are desperate.

I did all my hiring and promoting on gut feeling, and I still do. It's a mistake to ignore your gut, whether for team members or investors. This is especially the case in the early days when you might be looking for a co-founder, ceding your first piece of control. In that case, the gut feeling has to be 100%.

Hiring real superstars at the beginning makes super-scaling easier because someone can go off and develop a new idea, a whole new product, a new service, then lead it. If you hire the right person early on, that's your super-scaling done. One person with one brilliant idea can take you through to £20m-plus revenue, if a new service line is added or they lead a new geography. You can also grow quickly by moving people around into the next area of growth. The other side of this, however, is that mistakes in key early hires are costly.

Hiring for attitude out-trumps everything else and will mean that the pool of potential talent to be your future leaders will be as large as possible. When finnCap hired for attitude, our growth completely changed. We had some great people who came with no experience but with an amazing attitude, and accelerated their careers, but knowing what that attitude was, was vital. Senior hires have to be culturally aligned. Knowing that they are aligned reduces the risks of the hiring process later, because they will be hiring with the same values as you.

Once we got to a team of twenty people and around £3m revenue, we wanted to scale quickly to £10m, so the pace of recruiting new talent accelerated. You have to make sure people coming into the business at this stage are aligned because they are likely to be with you for another five years, and they will be recruiting people below them. If you hire the wrong people and they don't fit into your culture, at some point this will come back to bite you, and replacing them can be expensive, challenging and disruptive.

We asked questions like, 'Are you entrepreneurial? Have you got a fixed mindset? Have you got a growth mindset? Are you willing to challenge things?' A big question for us was, 'Do you absolutely love clients and love getting good outcomes for clients, rather than being driven by bonuses and money?' You need to find people who live and breathe your culture because, once you are over £3m, you will have a management team and reporting lines and it's less likely that you will all be in the same room together.

How the leadership role shifts as you scale

Once you grow to over fifty people, it's harder for you to have a direct impact on your individual teams. That's when it's particularly important to have recruited the right managers and trained them properly, and to have got everyone buying into the same vision in the same way.

Your main concern at this stage is to keep people motivated and energised (see the previous chapter). At this point, I started to read more about psychology than business strategy, and my key focus and area of learning became what drives people, and that transformed the way I thought about culture and helped us scale. I learned not to treat people as I thought they should be feeling, but to find out as much as I could about them to work out how they actually felt. This brought me back to our inclusive culture and how important it was.

Your culture will help you hire the people you need. As finnCap grew, and became known for being different in the way we looked after people, we were able to hire better people than might have been expected for the stage of development we were at, with people from bigger firms coming to us because they wanted a better culture. You still need to keep investing time and money in your hires, though, while constantly thinking ahead and planning for how you can best use them to grow.

The next level: Acquisition

Acquisitions are a great way to elevate your entire business, and the faster you acquire, the faster you can scale. They do come with lots of risk, however, and need to be made at the right time in your growth journey, and they need to be executed well. Bringing a culture that scales to a new acquisition requires a huge investment of time and energy, and even then it won't always work.

At finnCap, we scaled the business organically for twenty years, adding new divisions and teams and building market share in our chosen market. During that time, I looked at numerous acquisitions, some of them competitors and some add-on services, and I came close to acquiring, but didn't proceed because the businesses weren't right. Assessing potential acquisitions can be expensive if you spend money on advisers too early (acquisitions have a high risk of aborting at the last minute), so we spent very little money, only our time.

When we reached around £25m in revenue and approximately 5% market share, we knew that we could grow to around 10% market share, but to scale beyond that we would need to bring in another strategic service line: mergers and acquisitions (M&A). My chairman and I both felt that this was the right point to take some serious risk in order to acquire a decent-sized business with a known brand in M&A.

We therefore acquired Cavendish Corporate Finance, which at the time had a run rate of around £10m a year, for just over £14m. This added a new service for our clients and increased our presence in the private markets (not just quoted) with a well-known and respected brand. We completed this acquisition alongside an IPO in 2018.

Integrating the business was much harder and took longer than I had expected, because we had to apply our culture that scales to a brand-new team, and one that had existed as a team for a long time.

The work that needed to be done from scratch included:

- Setting out a new vision for the team

- Bringing our values to life and making them relevant to the new team every day

- Enrolling the team in equity participation and idea generation

- Engaging the team constantly in the way we worked and our culture, ensuring everyone was valued

- Making the changes to the team that were needed

- Recruiting new people with the right attitude and cultural alignment first, and elevating people into management roles quickly and at the right time, including the appointment of a new leader for the division (who went on to become my successor as CEO)

- Creating an exciting place to work and rewarding success

By committing to this intense programme, we succeeded in turning a £10m-revenue business into a division that achieved £24m turnover in the year ending March 2022. This was only possible using a culture that scales. Integrating an acquisition properly takes time, but it will lead to rewards in terms of growth.

The next level: Funding

Raising funds can transform and accelerate growth, and it is rare for a business to scale without outside capital. You are therefore likely to need to look at raising funds if you want to scale, either debt or equity.

This topic could fill a book in itself, but my key takeaway from years spent helping companies raise money, is that the most important factor for growth is to spend the time to find an investor whose vision matches your own. Gut feeling is crucial here. If something tells you an investor isn't going to work, listen to it. It will only become an issue much later, at which point it can be a big obstacle to growth but, much worse, it can cause the business to fail. You have to set out your vision clearly and honestly, and find an investor that buys into your vision, your timescale and you. Finding an investor can either transform growth or stifle it. If you find the right one, valuation will be much less of an issue. Go for the best fit, not the best valuation.

Summary

As elsewhere on your growth journey, you will have to make time for many conversations with people to fully understand them, even when you're busy and under pressure to generate revenue. Even if you have good managers, a lot of the thinking, planning and work to connect with individuals will fall to you. You will have to invest in coaching and training, but if you can make the most of your existing resources, you will avoid the need to replace people or make emergency hires, which are expensive on both an emotional and monetary level. Your team will have a culture that scales.

The best way to grow your team is to recruit great talent early in their career so that they grow with you over the long term, are aligned with your culture, and, when they reach leadership roles, will hire to the same values as you so that your next generation will be aligned with and engaged in your vision.

Listen to your gut when hiring and promoting, and focus on a candidate's attitude rather than their skillset. Focus on what you will need from them in the future, and whether or not they are a good fit for your culture, rather than whether they solve immediate problems. Think carefully about how to support people into management and leadership positions, including preparing their team for the promotion.

There are two routes to elevating your entire business: acquisition and funding. In both, it is crucial to invest time to secure the best fit for your vision and values, either from your acquisition or your investor. Again, trust your gut feelings and be prepared for the search to take a long time.

NINE

Exits: Slow Simmer

Introduction

Growing a business means constantly re-energising the team, which will also mean making changes to the team. It's important to keep building on existing capabilities by training current team members while also bringing in new people who have worked in bigger businesses and who have different skillsets.

In the previous chapter, we discussed how to make the most of your team's talents. Unfortunately, not everyone will stay with you for the whole of your growth journey – some of your team will reach their peak part way through, and others will simply not work out. Not making the decision to exit people is a barrier to growth. The wrong leaders will mean some divisions aren't growing, or will lead to a lot of staff churn. Being brave about decisions to exit people is key, and speed is important. It is hard – especially in the early days when you are a small, close-knit team – but it must be done if you want to grow.

One of the best pieces of advice I ever got was from my chairman of many years, who would say that, if you even start to think about someone not working out, it's already too late. I have kept that advice front and centre of my mind. It is easy to spend a long time trying to fix something that just isn't going to work, or ignoring a problem that you are finding difficult, but I have always felt great relief when a necessary exit is completed, and it always feels like the right decision afterwards.

That said, there is a way to manage departures to minimise upset, and sometimes that means getting the timing right to suit the individual. As long as you are aware of what you are doing, it is often better for your culture to wait a little longer for an exit. People sometimes choose to leave because they also know it isn't working, and that is a better outcome. As long as you are open and honest with people about the fit, their performance and any issues in a nice way, problems sometimes resolve themselves. Just don't stick your head in the sand. You will regret it.

Exits add to your alumni

Creating an external brand of being a good company to work for is a circular economy. It isn't just about looking after the people you have now. It's also about those who have left and what they say about you. Whatever happens, people will talk about your company just after they've left it. That's when they're the most likely to be negative about the company and potentially damage your growth.

On the other hand, your alumni are your potential future champions. Some go to competitors, some to investors, and some to suppliers, or, maybe five or ten years later, they become a client. I try to see everyone as a future supporter.

To maximise the potential of your future supporters, be careful about the impression they get of the company, right up to and including when they leave. If something goes wrong during their exit process that is still sitting with them and you don't acknowledge it, the anger will live with them for a long time and hang around when they are talking about you.

It is human nature that people who leave will say something about you once they've left, and you can't make sure that it will be something nice, but you can have a process that makes it less likely that any bad feelings will stick.

Make exits matter

How you exit someone is an important part of your culture and it says a lot about you and the company. At some point, you are going to have to let someone go, and it won't be easy. If it's not working for you, it's also not working for them, and it's important to understand why, even once it's over.

Anyone who has been through a divorce or a breakup knows that, later, things can be tricky if you are still angry. You might choose to spend time and effort in the aftermath, once the emotion is gone, trying to build a different relationship, or you might decide it's too difficult and move on. In business, your reputation depends on making the effort. Reputation is a long game. People who worked for finnCap are now on the boards of companies that give us work.

If it's a performance-based exit, you might be angry with that person and just want them out, and for the relationship to be over. It can be challenging when key people don't work out. Perhaps they have become disengaged, as we explored in Chapter 6, and an exit is the best solution, but you still want the person you are losing to be as positive as possible about you after they've left. Ask yourself how you will feel about the way you treated that person ten years down the line, when they might well be important to your business.

The most frightening and sensitive time for the person who is leaving is the few weeks after the exit. It will go a long way towards helping them heal if you follow up with them, see how they're doing, ask what you can do to help, make introductions. If you mean it, and if you're a nice person, their final impression of you (the one that they share) will be positive, with a sense that you have valued them.

Achieving empathetic redundancies

We have had people come to us after redundancies that had been handled badly, or had been a terrible shock, and it took them a long time to recover. I felt the impact every day, in their insecurity, and had to be conscious of this whenever I dealt with them. Some people never recover. Redundancy has the potential to cause huge mental health problems.

Finance, generally, has a hire-and-fire culture, and the constant threat of redundancy is part of that. You hear of a firm in which there is a round of redundancies every year, and another that loses the bottom 10%, and you think how awful it must be to work there. We try to avoid redundancy as much as possible at finnCap. We will only do it when the market is particularly difficult, and we have usually only had to have one round every three or four years.

In certain financial services firms, where redundancy is part of the culture, the process is clinical. People are paid, but there is little emphasis on having good discussions, which is how you can make someone understand why it's them and why it's not working, and why it's not personal. You can't do this perfectly every time. Not everyone will get it – some people will never get it, and will be angry with you for the rest of their life – but most people will appreciate your effort if you acknowledge the human side of redundancy, and are careful in how you talk to them and the time you give them to accept it.

Alongside this, you will have an HR process and a script that you are expected to stick to. When you're still small-scale, it's likely that you will call in some outside HR advice; you will be doing things by the book and it will all become clinical. If you go off script, HR will tell you that you're exposing the company to risk because someone can come back and sue you.

The law makes it hard to give people full explanations, but you can give some honest reasons. You might decide to take your own view on risk, which might not be the same as HR's. You will want to think about what this person's feelings about departing mean for your reputation, or your external culture. Are they a potential future supporter? What are they likely to say about you and can you change that? This means balancing the by-the-book advice with the human element of what's happening.

TOUGH TERRITORY: REDUNDANCY FOR GROWTH

After our buyout in 2007, we were hiring aggressively during a downturn, when no one else was hiring – if you want to accelerate your business plan, you need to hire better people than you can afford, and a downturn gives you a chance to secure the talent you need. Our cost base was going up, but the market hadn't recovered, so our revenue wasn't going up. I knew that, if the market didn't recover soon, I would need to cut costs. Hiring the person today that I needed for growth in the future would mean making someone else redundant in a year's time.

I felt that we couldn't pass up the opportunity to hire the people we needed to grow. By taking that stance, I was very much going against most of the management team at the time, and it was a lonely and tough position. By 2009, the market was terrible. We'd spent two years recruiting, accelerating our business plan, finding great people, incentivising them and getting them enrolled, but our cost base was too high. Although we'd hired better people, we weren't making any money. Directors took no salary for a while, but eventually 10% of the workforce had to go.

I'd never made redundancies on that sort of scale before. Making people redundant who, by then, felt like part of the family, was challenging. A CEO's job is to make those hard decisions, to protect everybody else within the business and maintain it. Would I like to keep everybody? Yes. Could we keep everybody? No. Did I know as I was recruiting that year that there was a good chance that I might have to lose some people? Yes.

However, the alternative is never to have an upgrade cycle of people coming in, which is not an option if you want to grow. All you can do is be true to your culture in the way you treat people.

The internal effect of exits

You need to explain to those who are not leaving why exits are happening. Carefully managing this message is important, especially after redundancies. Do it quickly, be clear about why it is happening, and be as open as possible. Talk to everyone together, be available to answer questions, and, to remove any uncertainty, make sure you can say that the redundancy process is complete and that no more will follow. If the right roles and people are made redundant, the effect on the team's energy will dissipate surprisingly quickly.

Senior exits

The more senior someone is, the more disruptive it will be to the business to remove them. Remember, however, that keeping a senior person who no longer fits is even more disruptive than removing them. The decisions about senior exits are harder, and you might be tempted to procrastinate. You also need to be even more careful about how you manage the process and how it will affect your reputation.

Growing businesses often need to re-calibrate after the initial excitement of the launch, when co-founders are no longer able to put in equal amounts of time, or when dynamics change as chairmen and key shareholders come and go. These are close relationships, and once you and they fall out of alignment, a lot of things stop working and you have to move on.

If you can keep communication flowing, be honest and open and do what you can to make the situation better, it is likely that your professional connection with the individual can survive. If someone knows you well and you have worked closely together, they should be able to see that you are trying, even if they are unhappy with the situation. If they can't see that you are trying, you'll probably never get to a better place with them. It's entirely possible that they will be rude about you for the first month or so after the exit, but once the emotion has left the situation, you might well be able to build a mutually beneficial relationship with them.

This also applies to non-executive directors and key shareholders. It's rare that you won't have some issues along the scaling journey, and you may need to make changes. Poor choices, incorrect fits or failing to act quickly when changes are needed can all stifle growth. Be mindful of these key roles, and keep assessing whether or not they are appropriate for your current scaling aspirations. New board members and shareholders can re-energise and supercharge growth where needed.

Listening for your cue to exit

As a CEO, there will be a point at which you become tired. For me, it was at around twenty years. It's when you're not able to generate excitement or energy as easily as you once did, and you realise the business is taking too much from you. You might not have the required skills to take it to the next stage. This is hard. It is also necessary to manage your own succession and to recognise when the time is right, for both you and the business, to exit. Getting this wrong can be a big barrier to growth.

Here are some signs that might indicate you're approaching the moment to exit:

- You have been the Visionary since the beginning, but the business now needs an Integrator (see Chapter 4) to deliver the details of your big picture.

- You realise that you are reaching a new chapter in your career. Perhaps your 'why' is different, or you realise it can be achieved elsewhere.

- You have been thinking about succession ever since you started hiring, and you now have an ideal successor in place. This might be someone who has a different skillset to yours, and it might seem like the moment when they will be most beneficial to the business in the CEO role.

- You are becoming bored and restless and need new challenges.

- Your skillset no longer matches the skillset required for growth.

- You are too tired!

The culture you have created will be your legacy, and there are ways to keep it alive even when you are not the active CEO, for example as a non-executive board member or a shareholder. If you manage your succession and find the right person, someone who knows what's required to take the business to the next stage of growth, you will have done your job and allowed growth to continue. You will have found the person who can then keep adding to the secret sauce blend, before finally handing the recipe on to the next generation.

Summary

Decisions about exits are hard, especially with long-standing or senior team members, board members and shareholders, but not making the decisions will store up problems and block your growth. If you can keep the human aspect of the situation in view and continue treating people well, you will avoid most negative reputational repercussions. Treat all your alumni as potential future allies and make their last impression of you as positive as possible.

Have an eye on your own exit door long before you think you may need it so that you can design a succession that is appropriate for the business and that will continue the business' growth journey. Have the right board for the current stage of your growth journey, and always be looking for additions that may transform your business.

Conclusion

Creating an inclusive culture is hard work. You're always working in the background, always listening, taking things on board, assessing mood and reacting where necessary. If you do it well, no one will ever realise how much you do.

Dealing with people properly, having the hard conversations, spending time to understand who people are, all requires empathy and sucks up energy. It means keeping on with your core message, repeating yourself, not getting annoyed when it takes you away from generating business, taking it on the chin when people tell you you've got it all wrong. That's part of the CEO's job, and it's a hard part. Coming up with a strategy and a mission is easy by comparison. Understanding people and making them feel valued is the part of the job I love doing, and it's what made my years as CEO rewarding, but it's not for everyone. If entrepreneurship is like extreme sports, empathetic entrepreneurship is even more extreme. You need to get your breaks, your time out and plenty of support.

Not all entrepreneurs are naturally empathetic, and some in leadership positions today still struggle with this aspect of the role. If you accept that culture is central to growth, it might also seem important for those individuals to acquire more people skills, and for those who have the skills but who think they might not be able to lead to realise what a valuable secret weapon they already possess. Empathetic leadership is different, looks different and, to all those entrepreneurs, especially the women, who may not feel like the traditional CEO or entrepreneur, this is your time. A culture that scales is something that can used by every business, but it needs to come from the top and is not a box-ticking exercise. I hope that you have been convinced and will start making a meaningful difference to your people, your productivity and your growth.

It might be that you like the sound of everything you've read in this book, and can see the value in it, but can't imagine yourself doing it. If you are a CEO of a scaling business and you know you aren't a people person, it might be worth your investment to appoint someone at board level who is, in the near future if not now, or to invest heavily in developing this skillset.

It might be that you have firmly grasped the concepts in the book, and will make a success of this journey with your business, and become your own Secret Saucemaster, adding your own unique adjustments and tweaks to create an excellent and inclusive blend. You'll know how to use the recipe when you need to, when to dial the seasoning up and down, and you will use it to scale your business. You'll also be able to share it with your team.

Once you have mastered the recipe, it might be time to think about the icing on the cake – how can we pass on the secret sauce that we've developed? Good corporate culture is also about giving back. There are many ways to apply a culture that scales.

I'm excited by the potential of applying this approach to scaling as widely as possible, to social interventions and not-for-profits. In your community, you probably have something that works brilliantly and that solves a problem, but how do you scale it? How do you bring a culture that scales to what is already there and working well, and help it achieve even more impact? How can you encourage others to think about a culture that scales? This is when we give our accrued wisdom back to our communities, which means we have achieved true mastery of the secret sauce and we are starting to see that what works for our businesses can also work in the wider world, and what its wider impact can be.

Where do you start?

What gets measured gets done and helps you improve, so I have put together The Scaleup Scorecard, a key resource to show you whether you are ready to scale and what aspects of my 6E process you need to focus on first.

This set of Scorecard questions is designed to help you work out which areas of scaling should be prioritised and covers the whole 6E process. It will give you a score for each stage of the process and provide you with a customised report to help you focus and get the confidence to start scaling.

To access The Scaleup Scorecard, go to https://scaleupscorecard.scoreapp.com/ or scan this QR code.

To find out how I work with scaling businesses to find their unique recipe, contact me at: Sam@thinkfair.world

Resources

World Class Manager – online management courses: www.worldclassmanager.com

Insights Discovery® – Psychometric tool based on Jungian psychology: www.insights.com

Centre for Entrepreneurs: www.centreforentrepreneurs.org

Acknowledgements

Where do I possibly start with everyone who has helped me on my journey so far? This could take a while.

My mum and my grandma are two very strong women who have always made me think that being a woman, young and different, or just being me, should never stop me achieving what I want, speaking up and speaking out. They gave me an inner belief in always doing what I think is right, whether or not others agree. My sister, for being my best friend, always, role-playing two successful women for hours when we were young (Pat and Sue we were – and, yes, Pat Hayward, I always wanted to be just like you, making people feel valued and amazing!). Thanks to my dad, who always gives the best advice and keeps me grounded and able to see what is important, as well as for putting up with all those strong and a tad-opinionated females around the house. At least you have a good sense of humour!

Mr Pinkney, who first got me interested in economics and inspired my love of business. My best friend, Anne, who taught me early to speak out, and that maybe there's a different way to do things and a better way to treat people. My choirmaster, Peter Mitchell, who gave me my first work experience, where I got the bug for the City and finance. My grandpa, Gareth and Cathy Humphries, for letting me cover a sandwich run at the bakery once, and realising how to do things better – my first taste of entrepreneurship. KPMG, for being a brilliant first job. John Finn, for taking a chance on me at the beginning and making it so much fun – he was way ahead of his time, especially on diversity.

My all-time star teammate in the first ten years, Karen Knight (or Simper!), for making it the most fun. James Edgedale, Eddie Edmonstone and Mick McNamara, for being great teammates and helping orchestrate the buyout of finnCap. Leslie Kent (our property analyst), for coming up with a great name (and the team for choosing it), my unbelievable PA and friend, Michelle Woodger – just a legend in her own right and an utter believer in treating people properly. Jon Moulton, the best chairman ever, a committed supporter and the best mentor for over eleven years; we were lucky to have him and his vast experience. Tom Hayward, for being my first CFO and ex-KPMG buddy; I always told him it was almost a part-time job and he never forgave me (it obviously wasn't!). Rhys Williams, for helping shape the finnCap business and finding the best restaurants, Stuart Andrews who relentlessly helped scale the business and has integrity like no one else, something more unusual than it should be in financial services. Stevie Scott, Mickey Pallett, Sid Lall, David Horner, Richard Power, Simon Like and Ken Wooton, for investing in us and believing in doing something different. Andy Brough, for making the City an all-round better place and helping me along the way. Anthony Jenkins, for some amazing and transformational advice that I'll never forget, an important lunch with the best advice that helped me scale. My walking buddies, friends and the best unofficial advisers, Jo Santinon and Rosaleen Blair, who have always championed good culture, growth companies and good business. Rosaleen is the best CEO I have ever met. Such an inspiration.

Daniel Priestley, for helping me shape my ideas and giving me the confidence to write a book. Oli Barrett, for just being an all-round introducer, networker, supporter and encourager of all things entrepreneurial, and the most positive person I know. Emma Stroud, Paul Jepson, Michael Hayman and Nick Giles, for helping me overcome my fear of public speaking and actually start to like it. I couldn't recommend them more highly to anyone else trying to get better at this. Three special CEOs who I have met along the way who I trust more than most, who have believed in me and been kindred spirits along this lonely journey: Tom Moriarty, Alastair Mills and Simon Tucker. John Farrugia, for being the right successor at the right time as finnCap CEO, for believing in treating people properly and keeping that inclusive culture going – keep scaling! To the best coach ever, Geeta Sidhu Robb, you just can't get any better and she has been an unbelievable help in my scaling journey, as well as my two amazing CEO forums, my ex-EO forum and YPO for their guidance, honesty, encouragement and support. It's not easy to find such amazing people and I never want to lose them. My amazing friends who are always there to support and listen in good times and bad. Also, to Geraldine, without whom I couldn't have written this book. You are awesome! And lastly, to all finnCappers past, present and future.

The Author

Entrepreneur Sam Smith is the founder, former CEO and adviser to finnCap Group Plc.

Sam established finnCap in 2007, having orchestrated the management buyout of a small broking division of J M Finn & Co Limited, a private client stockbroking firm. By 2010, directors and employees had purchased the remaining 50.1% of the equity retained by J M Finn. In 2018, finnCap acquired Cavendish Corporate Finance, a leading UK M&A adviser, floated on AIM in 2018, and began trading as finnCap Group Plc.

Sam was the first female chief executive of a City stockbroking firm and has worked on over 200 transactions,

IPOs and secondary fund raisings. Under her leadership, finnCap became a leading advisory firm for the business of tomorrow. The sector specialist service offering ranged from ECM and IPO, to Plc strategic advisory, debt advisory, M&A, and private growth capital, as well as net-zero and sustainability consultancy services through investment in Energise. finnCap Group includes finnCap Capital Markets and finnCap Cavendish to form a market-leading strategic M&A firm that has a global reach through its membership of Oaklins.

Sam is now an adviser to scale-up businesses and a non-executive director on the board of Sumer Group Ltd. She is an adviser to the Scale Up Institute, the not-for-profit whose mission is to make the UK the best place in the world to start and grow a business, as well as a private equity backed professional services business aiming to be the UK champion of SMEs.

Sam actively champions investment for underrepresented groups including female-led businesses and is dedicated to demystifying financial jargon for entrepreneurs. Sam is also passionate about empowering young people and helping them develop essential life skills. She is spearheading a campaign for entrepreneurship to be integrated into the school curriculum, and works with organisations such as YourGamePlan, icanyoucantoo and Modern Muse to help create a fairer foundation for young people, irrespective of their background. Sam is part of the Government Taskforce on Women-Led High Growth Enterprises, supporting the next generation of female entrepreneurs. She is also on the advisory board for Everywoman, which champions the advancement of women in business, the University of Bristol and is also Patron to The Entrepreneurs Network.

Sam qualified as a Chartered Accountant at KPMG. Her awards include 2010 Business XL, 2009 Business XL, Power Top 50 – no 3 in the City, National Business Woman of the Future Award and the Top 100 Financial Rising Stars Award.

✉ Sam@thinkfair.world

in www.linkedin.com/in/sam-smith-01974918/